Frank Stella

Frank Stella

William S. Rubin

The Museum of Modern Art, New York

Distributed by New York Graphic Society Ltd., Greenwich, Connecticut

Library of Congress Catalog Card Number: 75-100684
The Museum of Modern Art
11 West 53 Street
New York, N.Y. 10019
© 1970 by The Museum of Modern Art. All rights reserved
Printed in the United States of America

Designed by Joseph del Gaudio

Contents

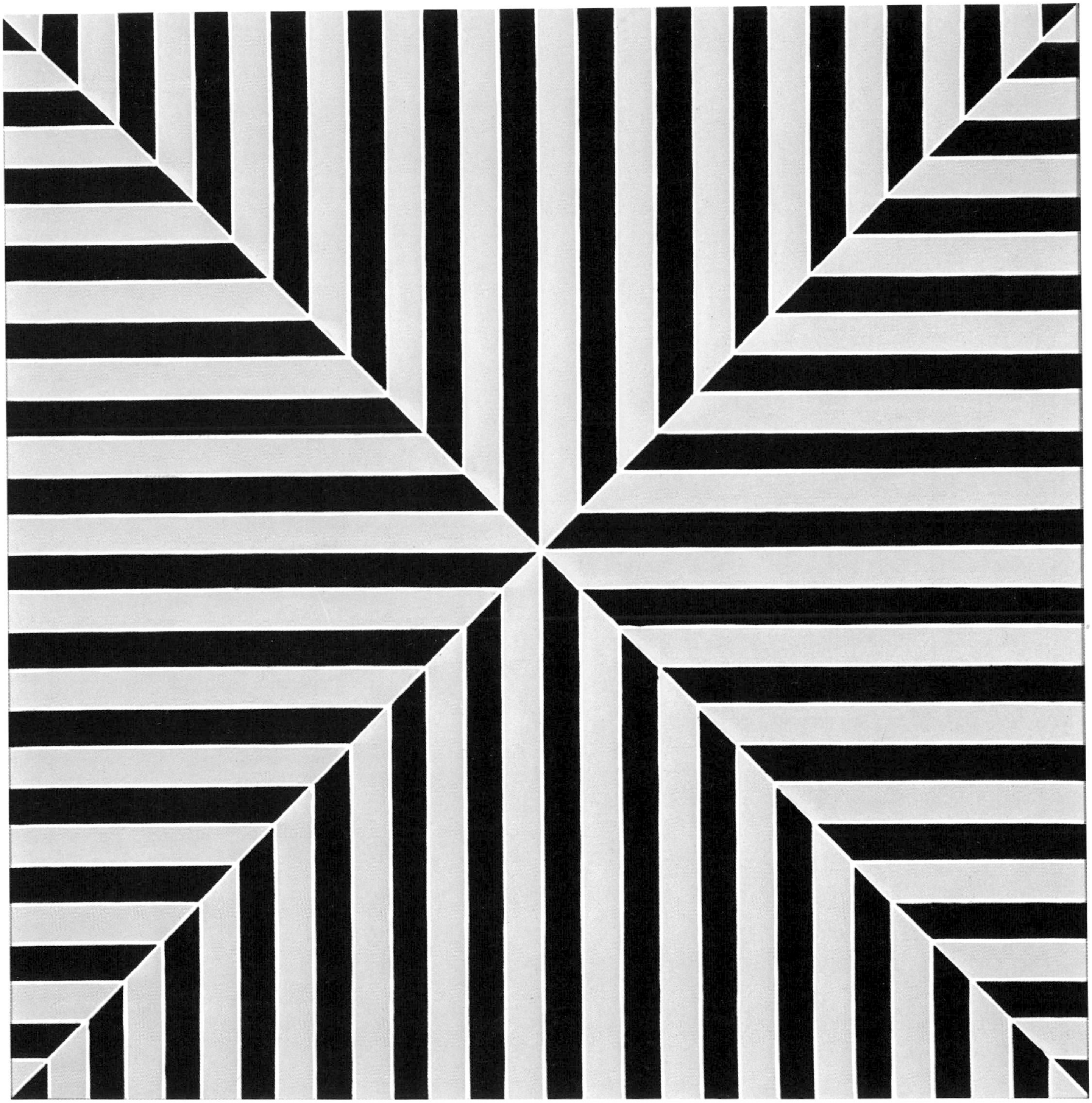

Marrakech. (1964)
Fluorescent alkyd on canvas,
6'5" x 6'5"

THE LATE 1950s heralded the public triumph of American avant-garde painting. The so-called Abstract Expressionists, previously overlooked or scorned by the public and the mass media, became celebrities. Their work, once bought only by a handful of friends and admirers (and fewer museums), found an ever-widening if less discriminating market. But the most convincing evidence of their impact on mid-century art was the almost frenetic manner in which their pictorial innovations were being adopted by younger painters all over the world.

Among the New York avant-garde, however, the near euphoria that had prevailed in the years following the war clearly began to disappear by the later 1950s. Ironically enough, at the very moment of its public triumph, Abstract Expressionism was experiencing a period of serious reappraisal and self-examination, not to say a crisis of conviction. When Frank Stella, having just graduated from Princeton, threw himself into the life of the New York art world in 1958, Gorky and Pollock were dead, Newman and Still had not shown publicly for seven years; and although de Kooning's style was being crudely imitated on every side, de Kooning himself was exhibiting only infrequently and had substantially withdrawn from the downtown artists community that he had dominated at the beginning of the decade. The art that Stella saw around him was less that of the original pioneers of the new American painting than that of a group of weaker artists—the "Tenth Street" or "second generation" painters—who had ridden the crest of Abstract Expressionism to the center of the scene in the mid-fifties.

By 1958 there was a feeling among some artists and critics that Abstract Expressionism had run its course. This impression was only partly justified, but it was certainly strongly reinforced by the proliferation of mediocre imitative painting being produced in Abstract Expressionism's name. Even those ambitious young artists who reacted against it, however, recognized that the masterpieces of the Abstract Expressionist generation provided the most immediate standard of real accomplishment against which to measure their own work. Nevertheless, the moment seemed propitious for change—the history of art seemed to be catching its breath. "Everybody was tired," Stella has recalled, "the field was sort of open. All you had to do was do it."[1] In a period in which many young painters were concocting pastiches of Abstract Expressionist styles, the authentic originality of Stella's art, and the conviction with which he pursued its premises, provided a new challenge for American painting. By the end of the decade, Stella had contributed to the already varied vocabulary of American art a style—and a concomitant approach to painting—that would, in the course of the 1960s, emerge as one of the few genuinely new paths for the continued development of major non-figurative art.

FRANK STELLA WAS BORN in 1936 in Malden, Massachusetts, a suburb of Boston. He has only vague recollections of the art classes in grammar school there, though he recalls sentimentally the demonstration drawings his teacher did on the blackboard—motifs such as the turkey at Thanksgiving time. Later, in junior high school, he became interested in the use of pastels, but he was rather put off by the technical aspects of conventional realistic drawing. "I wasn't very good at making things come out representationally," he recalls, "and I didn't want to put the kind of effort that it seemed to take into it." [2]

At Phillips Academy, Andover, Stella immersed himself in an extensive studio program that made a serious study of abstract composition possible. Indeed, Stella is one of the first major painters in the modern tradition to have been formed virtually entirely through the practice of abstract art. The artists of the Abstract Expressionist generation began to paint in the interwar period; as with the earlier European pioneers of abstraction, they were schooled originally in figurative painting. It is often claimed, of course, that an ability to draw and shade convincingly in a conventional academic manner is a prerequisite for good abstract painting. Some critics place a kind of moral value on representational competence, as if such competence guaranteed an artist's professionalism and gave him the right to be abstract. (Apologies have been made for abstractionists from Picasso to Newman to the effect that they can, after all, draw conventionally if they want to—as if that were the issue.) But in art only results matter. An artist needs only as much conventional "technique" as his form of expression demands. Many of the greatest masterpieces in the history of art have been created by men who were incapable of producing a conventionally realistic picture.

Stella's art teacher at Andover was Patrick Morgan—"He was just very interesting instead of very arresting" [3]—and the two got on well. "It was easy to get to know him, and he kept me working a lot." [4] Stella recalls that his painting at that time was strongly influenced—at least methodologically—by Morgan, who worked with a palette knife. Like Morgan, Stella frequently worked by scraping oil paint over a shellacked board surface. He painted a good deal during his Andover years. The school provided fairly generous studio space and an endless supply of free materials. The freedom that this situation engendered—a "mechanics of waste" [5]—encouraged Stella to try all sorts of possibilities "without nursing anything, not worrying about anything." [6]

In retrospect, Stella finds it interesting that many of his pictures at the time were organized in rectangles. "I got the point of Mondrian right away—or at least I got a point about him. I liked it, and I liked organizing things in blocks, abstractly. I thought about that, and often said that I wanted to paint just squares or something comparable. It seemed to me the thing to do; a painting could just be involved with squares, and that would be enough."[7]

It was Stella's good fortune to have arrived at Princeton during the tenure of Professor William Seitz. A former painter himself, Seitz taught art history at Princeton, but he also established a non-credit open studio course for interested students. Not long after Stella's arrival, Seitz succeeded in making painting an accredited part of the academic program, and a system of visiting artists was established. Stephen Greene taught at the university during Stella's last years.

Seitz, who had written his doctoral dissertation on Abstract Expressionism, and Greene were very much a part of the New York avant-garde. Stella went frequently to exhibitions in the city, and his discussions with Seitz and Greene about the art he was seeing—quite apart from their criticism of his own work—helped him clarify his feelings and ideas. Stella was majoring in history and took a number of courses in the history of art. He wrote his Junior research paper on Hiberno-Saxon illumination—a not unprophetic subject for an artist whose work was to be characterized by its geometrical complexity and linear intricacy. In his essay, Stella compared Pollock's painting with the all-over patterning characteristic of Hiberno-Saxon manuscript illuminations and suggested that neither of these apparently decorative linear styles had anything essentially in common with real decoration.

At Andover, Stella had painted rather geometrical pictures in small formats. Under the influence of Seitz and Greene, and as a result of the excitement he experienced in seeing advanced painting in New York, Stella was converted to a form of Abstract Expressionism.

I was very taken with Abstract Expressionism, largely because of the obvious physical elements, particularly the size of the paintings and the wholeness of the gesture. I had always liked house painting anyway, and the idea that they were using larger brushes . . . seemed to be a nice way of working. . . . Painting in that way I was as facile as the next guy, if not more so. I could "throw it around"; I wasn't inhibited about making a mess or losing control of a painting.[8]

Stella's development during his Princeton years (and afterward) profited considerably from the dialogue he established with Darby Bannard, one of the two other students in Seitz's painting class. Bannard shared Stella's regard for Abstract Expressionism, but he held back from it in his own work. "He didn't see any great virtue in being all out," Stella recalls,

and at the time I was overconvinced or overinvolved, in the sense that I thought I saw more than I see now in Abstract Expressionism—I mean, not so much in specific works as in the implications of the method and the way of working. It seemed like a real kind of breakthrough, and in a way, it was. . . . I still feel rooted in Abstract Expressionism—or New York School—as I probably always will be. It interests me as the painting I was formed around. I see it a little differently now and I began to see it differently then— What I saw, what I liked, was the openness of the gesture, the directness of the attack. . . .[9]

UNTIL STELLA'S LAST months at Princeton he painted in a vein derived from de Kooning, Frankenthaler, and Kline (his covers for the *Nassau Lit* especially recall the latter). He subsequently absorbed influences derived from Gottlieb and Motherwell (whose *"Je t'aime"* series he admired and, after graduation, parodied in a series of his own).[10] At the very end of his Princeton career, however, Stella entered on a period of rapid development in which he produced compositions containing single or multiple box forms placed in varying contexts of bands or stripes. These pictures constitute the bridge, or transition, to the Black series, in which his profile as an independent painter was convincingly established. The titles of these transitional pictures have no single source, but many—such as *Coney Island* (page 11) and *Astoria* (page 14)—reflect Stella's excitement with the ambiance of New York City, where he installed himself in a loft on Eldridge Street after leaving college.

In *Coney Island* a blue rectangle floats on a field of alternating red and yellow horizontal bands. Though the picture was realized improvisationally and contains some of the overpainting and scumbling that Tenth Street painting had appropriated from de Kooning, the picture's suspended rectangle reflected Stella's interest in the more simple, geometrically organized compositions of the post-1949 Rothko. ("I liked Rothko's softness, bulkiness, the one image—the presence and power of the one thing," recalls Stella, "but at the beginning, I didn't realize the full implications of his painting.")

Astoria represents a stage beyond *Coney Island* in Stella's transition, since the geometrical forms have been overpainted to produce a design made up entirely of horizontal bands. Much of the power and tension of the picture derives from visible evidence of the conviction which Stella needed to paint out the original composition in favor of this extremely simple and less visually "engaging" motif: in the interstices of the yellow bands, the black and chartreuse that formed the earlier pattern show through. The yellow has varying degrees of opacity over the surface, and this, combined with the other familiar elements of Abstract Expressionist painterliness, recalls Tenth Street painting, particularly that of Al Leslie, who had worked with irregularly placed bands of color spanning the canvas.

But the influence of painters such as Rothko or Leslie was, at this crucial stage in Stella's development, clearly secondary to that of Jasper Johns, whose first Flag, Target, and Number compositions date from 1954. There had been talk about Johns in the art history department at Princeton in the course of 1956–57. At that time, however, Stella had not seen any of Johns's work, not even in reproduction, and he found it a curious experience to speculate about an art that for him "didn't exist." "I had never seen it, but yet it was a kind of palpable reality of some sort that was in the air. . . . It was interesting to hear about something strongly reputed to be good, and then actually see it be good." [11]

Stella first saw Johns's pictures in January 1958, at Johns's first one-man exhibition in New York. "The thing that struck me most was the way he stuck to the motif. . . the idea of stripes—the rhythm and interval—the idea of repetition. I began to think a lot about repetition." [12] One night not long afterward, Steve Greene came into the studio in Stella's absence and, struck by the resemblance of his student's new pictures to Johns's Flags, scribbled "God Bless America" across the top of one of them. Furious at his teacher's temerity in defacing a painting, Stella didn't speak to Greene for some days.

While repetition of stripes parallel to the framing edge was the feature of Johns's work that most impressed Stella, it seems clear in retrospect that Johns's pictures of the fifties had other aspects that would relate to Stella's development. The particular painterliness of Johns's pictures would find some echo in Stella's Black pictures as—more importantly—would his emphasis on monochromy. Also of crucial importance in Johns's painting at that time was a unique relationship between his subjects and formats. Although he was clearly a representational painter, the motifs he chose—Flags, Targets, Letter and Number grids—were in themselves flat; this led to the possibility, realized in the Flags and Number grids, of making the field of the motif identical with the field of the canvas. That is to say, the Flag was not represented as an image *in* a pictorial field, but constituted the pictorial field itself. [13] Allowing the image or motif to determine, as it were, the outer contours of the picture had obvious implications for the later "shaped canvas." Indeed, as we shall see, Stella's first shaped pictures, the Aluminum series, depended upon just this kind of identification of field-shape and motif.

The flatness of Johns's motifs contrasted with the space-implying chiaroscuro of his painterly manner. But that aspect of his work interested Stella less than the patterning. The painterliness of Stella's Black series resulted from a simple facture that challenged the actual flatness of the picture surface much less than did that of Johns. This is not to imply that Stella felt any value as such inhering to flatness—any more than it inheres to space in other styles. But while flatness has nothing to do with the quality of a picture, it has much to do with its character. In the facture of his Black pictures, and more urgently afterward, Stella sought a directly given experience—an immediacy, simplicity, frankness, even bluntness—that would have been ill-served by such suggestions of finessed brushwork and painterly illusionism as remained in Johns.

The box-and-stripe pictures that Stella began in his last months at Princeton marked the beginning of his reaction against Abstract Expressionism. As already noted, these pictures were still arrived at improvisationally, with considerable reworking as the boxes and stripes were painted out or readjusted in the composition, leaving a residual impasto that was soon to disappear from Stella's pictorial vocabulary. Their formats, however, were pointing toward the symmetrical and heraldic configurations of the Black pictures which Stella began a few months after his arrival in New York.

Stella's emotional and critical reaction at this time against what he considered rhetorical in the Abstract Expressionist posture was more marked than the gradual mutation of his style suggests. "I think I had been badly affected by what would be called the romance of Abstract Expressionism," Stella recalls,

particularly as it filtered out to places like Princeton and around the country, which was the idea of the artist as a terrifically sensitive ever-changing, ever-ambitious person—particularly [as described] in magazines like Art News and Arts, which I read religiously. It began to be kind of obvious and . . . terrible, and you began to see through it. . . . I began to feel very strongly about finding a way that wasn't so wrapped up in the hullabaloo, or a way of working that you couldn't write about . . . something that was stable in a sense, something that wasn't constantly a record of your sensitivity, a record of flux.[14]

One aspect of Abstract Expressionism that particularly troubled Stella was the ambivalence artists felt about considering a picture finished, an attitude associated primarily with the "open-ended" aspect of the picture-making process espoused by de Kooning.[15] As Stella gradually telescoped his methods, eliminating improvisation on the canvas itself, the concept of the finished picture as the realization of a pictorial idea—good or bad—ceased to be problematic. (To some extent, the metamorphosis of a central idea in a single painting would be recaptured by its embodiment in a group of pictures constituting a series.)

IN NEW YORK CITY, Stella began to increase the size of his box-and-stripe pictures. He stretched the cotton duck over 1x3's which he butt-ended together.

14

Astoria. (1958)
Enamel on canvas, 8'½'' x 8'1''

This method, used for reasons of economy, produced an approximately 3-inch-deep stretcher that set the picture more clearly off from the wall.[16] Stella soon found this deep stretcher to his taste aesthetically and has retained the device. Given the flatness of his painting, there was always the possibility that the plane of the picture might be assimilated to the wall. The deep stretchers, he has remarked, "lifted the pictures off the wall surface so that they didn't fade into it as much. They created a bit of shadow and you knew that the painting was another surface. It seemed to me to actually accentuate the surface quality—to enhance the two-dimensionality—of the painting."

In view of Stella's eschewal of pictorial allusions to anything outside the painting itself—or even of illusionist references to the space of that extra-pictorial world—it was inevitable that the deep stretcher would focus attention on the picture as an object. And, indeed, that objective sense of the surface reinforced the anti-illusionist flatness. But in popular criticism the awareness of the object nature of the picture led in time to loose theorizing—on the level of what Meyer Schapiro has called "night-school metaphysics"—about the concreteness or objectness of the paintings. This kind of theorizing later played a role in the "justification" of Minimal art, and Stella feels it has turned into cant. "It's a little bit my own fault. I didn't mean it to be that way. I used to say that, after all, a painting is only an object—not meaning that it's just any object. It is a special kind of object—one that's intended to be a painting. My position was a reaction to the high-flown rhetoric of the fifties, but my reasoning got . . . abbreviated." In this regard, the net effect of the deep stretcher, Stella has observed, is that "it makes the picture more like a painting and less like an object by stressing the surface."

During his first six months in New York, Stella worked three to four days a week as a house painter.[17] His own pictures were painted with tint colors—a pasty pigment that house painters use to tint their neutrals—and with commercial black enamel. This, like his use of the butt-ended stretcher, was mainly an economy measure. "It was like having a lot of oil paint; for thirty-five cents you could get a quart of it and you could do a lot of painting."[18] He frequented the cellars of the paint dealers on Essex Street, buying decorator colors that had gone out of fashion for a dollar a gallon. Stella liked those purples, purple-reds, and chartreuses, and "in a way, a lot of problems were sort of solved. You could get only certain kinds of colors and thus certain kinds of things were given—so I worked with those."[19]

We have seen that after experimenting with numerous combinations of stripes and boxes, placing the latter in different positions, Stella arrived at pictures that contained only rows of horizontal bands. At first, the all-band pictures contained traces of improvisational impasto underpainting, particularly in the interstices of the bands. But once Stella decided to work exclusively with bands, he began sketching his design beforehand, executing the stripes without reworking the surface.

In the course of 1958 Stella simplified his designs yet further and at the same time reduced the range of his color. He had already been using a good deal of black along with the tint colors. In a few paintings where he "got into trouble" with the color, he simply overpainted the problematic areas in black and thus produced his first all-black pictures. In *Delta* (page 17), for example, the black bands are set off by traces of an earlier red painting that remains in the interstices. (Unlike most of the transitional pictures, *Delta* has a somewhat complicated pattern, anticipating that of *Turkish Mambo* of the following year [page 36] and other later paintings in the Black series.) The reduction to black temporarily shelved the problem of color juxtaposition and allowed Stella to concentrate on design and structure. His first four series of paintings, which included the pioneering shaped canvases, were all monochromatic. Only three years later would he once again confront the problem of color.

ONE BY ONE the various components that characterize the Black series (pages 19–43) were being established. The decision to cover the entire field with bands was followed by the gradual opening of a space between them. In the Black pictures the parallel 2½-inch stripes or bands of black enamel are painted at a slight distance from one another, allowing a very narrow strip of unpainted canvas to show in between. This practice had evolved out of the more heavily impastoed transitional works: as Stella overpainted and reworked the bands of color in those pictures, he consciously refrained from making the later layers of adjoining bands totally contiguous by stopping the new color short of the edge of the bands underneath. This created a less defined edge and a kind of "breathing space" between the bands. In time, the bands became increasingly separated, more autonomous, and when Stella embarked on the Black paintings, he planned the pictures with narrow unpainted spaces between them.

The optical effect of the value contrasts between the painted black bands and these reserved interstitial unpainted strips led many journalists to speak of "white pin-stripes," especially when they had only seen photographs of the paintings; and this, in fact, became a term of opprobrium that received some currency in the popular press. Stella attacked the characterization with a tongue-in-cheek letter to *Newsweek*:

Outside the perimeter of my affections and activities . . . an enterprise known as "white pin-stripe painting" seems to be gathering momentum. I wish to dis-

claim your blundering attempt to include my name in the roster of this new school of painting.

My own work . . . uses fairly broad stripes of black, and, more recently, aluminum or copper paint.

I have never seen a "white pin-stripe painting" . . .

. . . there is a distinction between what any artist DOES, and what he does NOT do; and however it may lack journalistic appeal, this boundary is precisely the necessary limit without which no work of art can exist. With respect to my painting the case seems particularly simple: it is an observable physical fact that I have laid down paint in certain spaces, and have not done so in others.

Those who battle for the claims of "taste" should remind themselves occasionally that the arts are based upon concrete data. . . .[20]

Stella's insistence that he had not painted white lines followed from the importance he attached to not *drawing* with the brush—the method that had been crucial to most Abstract Expressionists. "I didn't like the Abstract Expressionists' use of drawing," Stella recalls,

because of its modeling and value-difference implications. But I think their instinct to put skeletal and gestural drawing back into painting was shrewd and fruitful. It forced me (and everyone else) to think hard about the integral relationship of surface, structure, and painting methods. In a curious way this drawing-painting problem forced me into structural and spatial considerations. . . . I ended by only painting with the brush; I didn't do the drawing with it.

Nevertheless, Stella did do the drawing without it—inasmuch as the "negative" spaces between the bands really functioned as lines. Moreover, the edge of the canvas—which is "negative" in the sense that it demarcates one border of the outer bands—is thereby equated with the "negative" space that indicates their inside borders. This identification helps explain why the drawing *on* the surface would logically require that the drawing *of* the surface—i.e., the shape of the canvas—be brought into consonance with it. Stella's "negative drawing" accounted for the essential structure of his art through 1965, and even as his work subsequently expanded to include an increased role for color, his painting remained predominantly draftsmanly.

The tendency of the viewer to read the unpainted areas as the "positive" aspect of the design, to bring them up visually to the plane of the black, follows from the habit of seeing black as the shadow of forms—a habit formed more from looking at representational images than from looking at the world. In the Black paintings, the actual execution thus runs against the grain of optical expectation—a situation enhanced by the total absence of modeling and of all

"Die Fahne hoch." (1959)
Enamel on canvas, 10'1½" x 6'1"

View of installation at exhibition *Sixteen Americans*
The Museum of Modern Art, New York, December 1959–February 1960

but casual or accidental value variation in the paint. The result is a visual experience in which even such vestiges of illusionistic space as remained in Abstract Expressionist pictures—an inevitable by-product of their painterly draftmanship—have been largely expunged from the picture.

Stella began the Black paintings late in 1958. Although he had some sense of their constituting a group or series, he progressed from picture to picture without that comprehensive overview or acute sense of problem-solving that was to govern the Aluminum and Copper series. Not that he was unconcerned with solving plastic problems; indeed problem-solving became the essential dialectic of his development. In this case, he simply approached the process somewhat less systematically.

To be sure, all painters are problem-solvers, for all must bend the plastic structures they inherit to the expressive needs of a new age and a new personal sensibility. Among modern painters, this process has been somewhat more conscious and, hence, more a part of their dialogue with their art and with each other. Even as late as Abstract Expressionism, however, such pure plastic concerns played a comparatively small role in artists' discourse. But among the abstract artists of the more recent generation, the combination of a more rigorous exclusion of extra-plastic components, and of a less Romantic, hence less rhetorical posture, have contributed to a more single-minded address to these problems (a situation that has naturally encouraged a related mode of criticism).

The sketches of the Black pictures, made on drawing paper and yellow pads (graph paper only came later), set out the schemas of their emblematic patterns in a very summary manner.[21] Stella then painted the stripes freehand on the canvas. Sometimes he did not know how many bands the picture would contain. If the pattern was centralized—as in *"Die Fahne hoch"* (page 19) and the pictures with diamond motifs (page 33)—he would paint from the middle of the canvas outward and would discover how many stripes fitted onto the surface as the work progressed. Certain frame-paralleling motifs, such as that of *Tomlinson Court Park* (page 23), were painted from the outside toward the center. Each band was overpainted three or four times in order to create a paint film that would detach the band somewhat from the canvas texture. (Later, in the Moroccan series, Stella used a single coat to obtain a more transparent paint film and, in the Protractor series, stained the paint directly into the canvas weave.) Despite the fact that all his patterns were symmetrical and were made up of bands whose segments were straight, the freehand method produced effects that were anything but geometrical. Some Black pictures, such as *Turkish Mambo* (page 36), were in fact visibly lopsided; and in such a rigorously schematized picture as *"Die Fahne hoch,"* where at first glance all the bands appear to be strictly parallel to the edges of the field, close inspection reveals that they actually waver slightly.

Moreover, even when Stella began (in the Aluminum series) to pencil light guide lines for the stripes on the unpainted canvas, the actual execution, though more crisp, never took on the character of precisionist painting. The edge was always slightly irregular; the surface—never hard—was allowed to breathe, and no attempt was made to hide *pentimenti* or small accidents of execution. Stella's facture is thus totally alien to geometrical painting, though unhappily this did not prevent his work from being commonly, and mistakenly, associated with that manner on the basis of its rectilinear configurations (see below, p. 25).

A number of aesthetic choices apart from facture account for the profound difference between Stella's art and that of the geometrical painters. The most important difference follows from Stella's affirmation of what he has called "non-relational" painting. At the present remove, we can see that the so-called non-relational method of organizing a picture surface derives more from the synoptic character of all-over, holistic composition as explored by certain Abstract Expressionists than it does from anything in the geometrical tradition. In a lecture at Pratt Institute in 1960[22] at the time of the *Sixteen Americans* exhibition at The Museum of Modern Art, Stella spoke of needing to go beyond

relational painting, i.e., the balancing of various parts with and against each other. The obvious answer was symmetry[23]—make it the same all over. The question still remained, though, of how to do this in depth. A symmetrical image or configuration placed on an open ground is not balanced out in the illusionistic space. The solution I arrived at—and there are probably quite a few, although I know of only one other, color density[24]—forces illusionistic space[25] out of the painting at a constant rate by using a regulated pattern.[26]

The relation between symmetry and the expunging of three-dimensional space was reciprocal, however, and Stella later observed that "if you're that much involved with the [two-dimensional] surface of anything, you're bound to find symmetry the most natural means."[27]

To apprehend what Stella means by "non-relational" painting, and the connection of this concept with certain stylistic aspects of the art of his immediate antecedents, some further explanation is necessary. Old Master illusionism demanded that the image work both laterally—as a patterning of forms on a flat surface—and in depth. The natural tendency of the viewer was to look *into* the illusion, but he perforce looked laterally *across* the surface. The two readings were reciprocal, and the compositional balance of the picture approached symmetry only when—other requirements met—its main elements were aligned in a single plane parallel to the picture plane, as in the painting of the High Renaissance. Even then, of course, the frontality and symmetry were only approximate, and the two sides were not interchangeable since the configurations were designed, however unconsciously, for the scanning of the picture from left to right.[28] Needless to say, any tendency toward bilateral symmetry was rarer in the more oblique compositions of the Baroque. It is not accidental that the most symmetrical configurations in older art are to be found not only where the content was most inherently hierarchical, but where the space—at least the tactile, sculptural space created by modeling and perspective—was most shallow, as in Byzantine and Romanesque art (or where it was purely schematic, as in Egyptian painting). Not that the frequent use of symmetry in these styles was determined by the same expressive ends as was the symmetry in Stella, though there are at least distant affinities: he, too, sought an iconic or heraldic presence in his Black paintings—a sense of unremitting stasis, and a configuration that could be instantly grasped, in the manner of older emblematic imagery.

23

Many painters in the modern tradition, beginning with Manet, consciously sought to create an illusion of shallower space and emphasized the two-dimensionality of the picture support by other surface-affirming devices. A lateral as opposed to a recessional reading of the image became more and more dominant. Cézanne, for example, modeled only the fronts of forms, "bleeding" them into one another (the basis of Cubist *passage*) and blunting perspective. He created images that might, in effect, be considered simulacra of bas-reliefs— as opposed, for example, to Renaissance paintings, which are comparable to sculpture in the round in a measured "stage" space.[29] As the modern tradition progressed, its language became increasingly abstract. The hierarchies of form on which older art was based became less and less central, although certain conventions of hierarchical or relational structure were still maintained even in high Analytic Cubism, where the abstract fragments were arranged to left and right of the axis to achieve a balance that depended upon compensatory, "relational" arrangements.

In Mondrian's paintings of 1913–14, where the hierarchies of unit size were approximately evened out, a configuration verging on bilateral symmetry was achieved. This was even more marked in certain of his pictures of 1918–19, where the last vestiges of conventional illusionistic space, still present in the 1913–14 pictures, were suppressed, and the configurations reached out to touch the frame on all sides.[30] Nevertheless, though the "relational" aspects of such compositions were reduced to minimal differences of accent—slight asymmetries in color placement, or discrepancies in the width of the black lines—these aspects still constituted the essential visual dynamics of the picture. However much abstracted, however subtle, comparable asymmetries and hierarchical distinctions continued to govern all post-Mondrian, geometrical art in Europe, whether that of the Abstraction-Création movement or that of the more recent Groupe de Recherche d'Art Visuel. Stella himself has observed that some of his own images and patterns can be found in the work of artists of these groups; but he also insists that their art "still doesn't have anything to do with my painting."[31]

The central reason for the difference Stella is insisting on here—aside from obvious factors such as size, scale, and shaped canvas—is that within the framework of the governing symmetrical patterns used by geometric painters, those subtle adjustments which gave pictures a "relational" aspect continued to be incorporated. Moreover, though no longer figurative, such pictures still invited the left-to-right scanning that has prevailed in most Western art, and which is rooted in narrative exposition.[32] Nineteenth-century modern painting tended to adjust itself to such a reading; the compositions were generally more open on the left and more closed on the right. Even though the Cubists and their descendents worked more with "iconic" than "narrative" configurations, the left and right were not interchangeable. If scanned in the manner of older pictures, Stella's absolute bilateral symmetry would produce a sense of *imbalance,* precisely because his configurations are not designed to be read across the picture. Stella's paintings—and those of certain of his contemporaries—force us to look in a different way; the apprehension of their balance demands an instantaneous visual grasp of their oneness.

In order to assure his absolute symmetry, Stella was compelled to force out of the picture the implications of illusionist space that were still present to varying degrees in geometrical painting. We have seen how his monochromy, his avoidance of modeling, his "negative pattern," and use of deep stretchers helped accomplish this. But as Clement Greenberg has observed, *absolute* flatness is possible only on an empty canvas.[33] A single line drawn on its surface is sufficient to compel some kind of spatial reading. Hence Stella had to confront the fact that though he had mightily pared down the suggestion of space, he could never totally abolish it. His solution was the "regulated pattern" which "forces illusionistic space out of the painting at a constant rate." In the end, it is the "constant rate" that is the key to the spatial equilibrium and thus to the symmetry. We might therefore recast Stella's statement by saying that "such inevitable vestiges of spatial suggestion as remain are kept at even depths by the regular pattern, hence maintaining the possibility of absolute symmetry."

Certain critics—a majority, in fact—have viewed Stella's work as primarily in the line of geometrical art. Opinion in this group has ranged from those who have seen him simply as going back to Mondrian,[34] to others who have admitted many differences—sometimes even more than Stella himself would care to recognize. "Geometric forms, it is discovered," wrote Max Kozloff of Stella and George Ortman, "can look lonely, express irony, confuse themselves with objects, mimic the monotonous, equivocate about space and contain, emanate or deny light in ways that suggest that there has been a rather shameful failure of invention [in the geometric tradition] up to now."[35] The problem of Stella's position is most easily resolved—it seems to me—by recognizing that he is not in the historical line of geometrical painting at all. He derived from Abstract Expressionism and evolved out of it. Rather than continuing the "researches" of geometrical art (as exemplified, for example, by Vasarely), he gradually came to impose a regularized patterning upon the energies of holistic Abstract Expressionism, and much of the power of his painting has grown out of the tension produced by these divergent tendencies. His "order" was not established a priori but was achieved by working, in effect, against the grain of his own first instincts.

In this way, an ambiguous, apparently geometrical, order was ultimately created by an artist who admittedly "couldn't draw a straight line, or build a stretcher with a right angle."

Thus the immediate predecessor of Stella's "non-relational" image is to be found not in the geometrical tradition but in the all-over style of Pollock and the related configurations of Rothko and Newman. The synoptic, holistic character of Pollock's poured pictures depended on suppressing traditional hierarchies of size in favor of an approximate all-over evenness in the pictorial fabric. The similar all-over distribution of color, which averaged out into a tonal whole, and the more or less even densities of pigment dosage, assured a web which would be biaxially symmetrical and frontal and situated in a space that—however it might be read[36]—would suggest an approximately even depth throughout. Rothko's characteristic configurations also combined frontality, lateral symmetry, and an elusive but approximately even depth, while in Newman the image was frontal, but the symmetry was usually vertical rather than lateral. In many of Newman's paintings the holistic quality was guaranteed by the single color of the field and by the fact that the vertical bands passing through the field resonated and articulated that color more than they divided or shaped it. Newman's minimizing of "visual incident," his rectilinear format, and his less painterly facture anticipated the manner of Stella, while the all-overness of Pollock foreshadowed Stella's synoptic, biaxially symmetrical configurations.

The advantages of the holistic or, as it also came to be called, "single-image" structure that emerged in the late forties and fifties were its synoptic immediacy and its boldness of visual impact. The structure combined the strong unity and simplicity of its configuration with constant, relatively limited local variations, such as the varying densities of the skeining in Pollock or the value gradations from point to point within a single color area in Rothko. In Stella's early years at Princeton, it was the powerful directness of Abstract Expressionist art that had appealed to him, although his sense of the style was then based primarily on de Kooning, Kline, and their followers. By the time Stella began the Black pictures, this vein of Abstract Expressionism—as distinguished from that of Pollock and Rothko—had begun to seem labored to him, to suffer from a kind of mannerism, especially around the edges of the compositions. Typical exponents of the style, Stella recalls,

often seemed to me to have found one part of the painting that they really liked—one part where it worked—and then spent the rest of their time . . . trying to nurse the painting into a situation that would show off and embellish the one good part of their painting to its best effect. . . . I didn't want to be involved

The Marriage of Reason and Squalor. (1959). Enamel on canvas, 7'6¾" x 11'¾"

26

in the kind of painting that was mostly correctional . . . trying to nurse something that was supposed to be fresh and direct to begin with. . . . the whole revisionist aspect of most abstract painting in the later fifties was a real problem. . . . [it] got into a lot of muddy situations.[37]

It was then that the importance of Pollock's all-over style began to be clear to Stella. While he was at Princeton he had seen relatively little work by Pollock in the original, despite his discussion of that artist in his essay on Hiberno-Saxon illumination ("Pollock wasn't that available around '57 or '58"), and he had arrived at the aesthetic of his Black pictures with little sense of relation to Pollock's art. Only as he was about halfway through the Black series—not until "it was literally staring me in the face"—did he begin "to see the importance of Pollock—what it was really about—and the difference between Pollock and the more typical Abstract Expressionists."

The classic Pollock image, with its holistic symmetry and its all-over fabric, reinforced by a technique that precluded a priori the finesse of the hand still favored by most Abstract Expressionists, seemed to Stella to be more direct and to represent a more unequivocal break[38] with the vestiges of figuration that were continually resurfacing in most Abstract Expressionist compositions. "I was very bothered," Stella observes

by the obvious academic art-school heritage of Abstract Expressionist painting —especially the use of a large brush loaded with paint in such a manner that it had the same effect as a piece of charcoal. Pollock seemed to me to have put painting and drawing together in a really sensible way, i.e., to have cut down the ambiguous gap that lingered on in so-called Action Painting between the studies and preparation for a picture and its actual execution. Instead of drawing with paint, Pollock could paint with drawing, thus raising the whole level of gesture, making sense of the possibility of real gestural painting. Pollock made it a lot easier to see this, and particularly to see it in subsequent painters like Louis. Of course it's an obvious line of development now, and it was per-haps fairly obvious even then, but to see it wasn't that easy.

The general sense of crisis that pervaded abstract painting in the late fifties— the rise of Neo-Dada and the putative widespread "return to the figure"—put practitioners of non-figurative art on the defensive. "To an art student in those years, it seemed to need to be defended. And Pollock was one of those who was easiest to defend it with," Stella recalls.

His drip paintings represented a kind of dramatic breakthrough—and a kind of breakdown. . . . Pollock really made it impossible to go backward in terms of figuration and thinking. He made it really necessary for you to think about abstract painting: to think through it, and think ahead with it. In other words, he made your commitment—you didn't have to worry about where you stood. Pollock had sort of done that for you. You had an open vista, but you couldn't go back at all. . . . You had to find your own way.

Despite the relationship of Stella's Black pictures to all-over, holistic painting, the differences between them are as great as the similarities—and much more obvious. While Pollock gained visual impact and immediacy from the oneness of his web, his image included countless local hierarchies and surface variations, which established the rhythm of expansion and contraction—the "pneuma"—of the composition. The same kind of coexistence of extremes characterized Rothko: at one end of the expressive spectrum, the monumental and simple configurations; and at the other, the refined local surface variations that endowed the work with intimacy. In the case of Pollock, and even that of Rothko, there were vestiges of Analytic Cubist space.[39] And beneath the expression of improvisational freedom and meandering anti-tectonic drawing which characterized the Pollock surface was a sense of structural coalescence that reflected an implicit architectural order elliptically dependent—as it was more obviously in other all-over styles—on the infrastructure of the Cubist grid.[40] Stella tried for a different kind of all-overness—uninflected and disengaged from any implications of the Cubist grid. "I tried for something which, if it is like Pollock, is a kind of negative Pollockism," Stella suggests. "I tried for an evenness, a kind of all-overness, where the intensity, saturation, and density remained regular over the entire surface."

This new evenness required that Stella carry the governing pattern right out to the frame of the rectangular field, just as it would soon require that the shape of that framing edge be locked to the surface pattern in an ineluctable reciprocity. The webs of Pollock, like the rectangles of Rothko on their lateral sides, had stopped just short of the edge of the field, and had existed in the vestiges of a shallow "relief" space—both factors reminiscent of Analytic Cubist structure. Only Newman's "zips" had entirely spanned the fields of the pictures. As Stella flattened the space, regularizing it by the serial character of the patterns that he chose, he usually made the bands either touch the framing edge or recapitulate its right angle.

This simultaneous flattening of the space and carrying of the configuration to the edge echoed, at a considerable remove, the development of Cubism from its Analytic to its Synthetic phases. But Synthetic Cubist compositions were more developed in the center of the field, thus re-enacting and implying by what we may call quantity of visual incident what had earlier been carried by the relief structures of Analytic Cubism. Moreover, the congruence of the straight lines and the framing edge was only approximate in Synthetic Cubism, whereas Stella's black bands more closely paralleled the framing edge or paralleled the diagonals implied by its four corners. Only in Mondrian's paintings of 1918–20 (and in the geometrical art influenced by Mondrian) do we find configurations closely approximating those of Stella; but as has already been observed, even these introduced—either in the plotting of the colored squares or in the subtle variations in thickness in the lines—asymmetrical cross relationships which Stella would reject as "relational." (Mondrian's post-1920 configurations, despite their continued paralleling of the framing edge, are at an even further remove from Stella's frame-locked compositions.)

In isolating from all-over painting the bold unified fabric at the expense of its local variations, Stella was intent on making the visual experience one of instantaneous apprehension. The power of his pictures derived from the clarity and speed with which their patterns—and later their entire shapes—"stamp" themselves out retinally, as Michael Fried puts it.[41] Fried's verb is well chosen, for Stella himself has spoken of a rubber stamp—as he has of a cooky cutout—in describing the "visual imprint" he sought to achieve. "I wanted something that was direct—right to your eye . . . something that you didn't have to look around— you got the whole thing right away."[42]

By eliminating the local visual incident of all-over painting in order to deliver his immediate "visual imprint," Stella was functioning in a manner characteristic of many modernist innovators who have created new visual experiences by sacrificing elements of the plastic language of their predecessors. Most critical writing stresses the reductionist aspect of this dialectic rather than its effect of opening the pictorial situation to more far-reaching possibilities within the conventions that are retained. Stella finds "something awful about that 'economy of means.' I don't know why, but I resent that immediately. I don't go out of my way to be economical. . . . I don't think people are motivated by reduction. . . . I'm motivated by the desire to make something, and I go about it in the way that seems best."[43]

Nevertheless, given the historical context in which Stella's early pictures made their appearance, it is not surprising that even serious criticism could refer back to his "stupefying austerities."[44] The degree of this austerity derived only in part from the limitation to black in large-size works—which was, in any case, not without precedent, e.g., Picasso, de Kooning, Pollock, Newman, Reinhardt, and Rauschenberg. Nor was it primarily a question of facture, for although Stella rejected the painterliness and rich impastoes of Abstract Expressionism, his surfaces were decidedly less austere than those of geometrical painters or the hard-edge painters, such as Ellsworth Kelly. The austerity had mostly to do with visual incident. Not its quantity—since much less "went on," so to speak, in a Newman painting—but its regularity: Stella's use of serial patterns which formed simple emblems.

That an artist could presume to make a picture from such obvious configurations as did Stella in his earlier works angered even critics who had accepted Abstract Expressionism. One, for example, wrote that "the main characteristic," of Stella's paintings was "total indifference. Valueless as art . . . a perversion of the function of art by using its formal repertoire to deny the possibility of feeling. . . . These paintings are semi-icons for a spiritual blank. They make Mr. Stella the Oblomov of art, the Cézanne of nihilism, the master of *ennui*."[45] "It is now a little difficult," wrote another regretfully some years later, "to summon up again the incredulity and ridicule (my own included) with which these works were greeted."[46]

Such negative critical reactions have of course met almost every new phase of modern painting since its inception, and while critical attacks hardly constitute guarantees of authenticity for the art being criticized, the history of the last hundred years suggests that the greatest vehemence has been aroused primarily when plastic conventions were being most profoundly challenged. This history also seems to imply that the *quality* of modernist art is inexorably bound to the fact of this challenge in a way that was not true of the Old Masters.[47]

To those for whom the paintings of Stella spoke at that time with an authentic voice—or those who have since discovered this voice—the pictures have not the spirit of nihilism or negation but of affirmation. To be sure, the affirmation of certain experiences—the making of choices—constitutes an implicit negation of others, but this applies to Stella no more than to artists of the past. No emotions are less "human" than others; all are equally available to the purposes of art. Even ennui can be turned into the substance of major art, while the "noble" emotions can and have provided more than their share of failed painting. The criticism quoted above not only confused Stella's supposed subject but equated it with his quality. Indeed, to be the "Cézanne of nihilism"—to give Cézanne's density of aesthetic order to any human attitude—would be quite an accomplishment.

On the plastic level, the simple, serial character of Stella's earlier motifs are of admittedly limited expressiveness in themselves and are thus resistant to the purposes of art. Part of Stella's power derives from his having made high art of such intractable matter. It was a risk comparable to that of the Cubists restricting themselves to fragments of geometry or Matisse to the constituents of decoration. When using such motifs, the artists of the Groupe de Recherche d'Art Visuel handle them equivocally and artily; in this they proclaim the limits of their work. Stella's more direct and uncompromising use of these materials announced a greater ambition. He is, in fact, one of the very few painters to have emerged in the late fifties and sixties who shares with the early pioneers of modern art, and with the major Abstract Expressionists, a spirit of immense ambition. Had he failed, his failure would have been utter and absolute.

STELLA'S BLACK PICTURES divide roughly into two groups: those painted during 1958 and through the fall of 1959, and those dating from the winter of 1959/60. In the earlier group, the black bands are all rectilinear and parallel to the framing edge. *Tomlinson Court Park* (page 23) is the most closed of these compositions in the sense that each of its concentric rectangular bands simply parallels the frame. They do not recapitulate it exactly, however, since the proportions of each rectangle change, elongating as they move toward the center of the field. *"Die Fahne hoch"* (page 19) is maximally open; in each of its four quadrants the bands begin and end at the frame. Both these pictures have a biaxial symmetry. *The Marriage of Reason and Squalor* (page 27), on the other hand, is symmetrical only on its vertical axis, its binary form constituting, in effect, a mirror-image pairing of the configuration. In none of these paintings is the symmetry exact, however, since they were all painted freehand from sketches that were less fully elaborated than were the graph-paper studies for later works.

This is, of course, the way Stella wanted it. Not only did he wish to avoid the mechanical appearance of the truing and fairing of geometrical art, but he wished frankly to reveal the tracking of the brush with whatever awkwardness that might entail. Such an approach constituted for him more than an affirmation of anti-elegance; it revealed an insistence upon the importance of the *conception* of the picture as opposed to the refinements of its *execution.* "I feel that it's the over-all effect of the painting that counts," he observed a few years ago.

The painting must convince you on that level, rather than by technical niceties, particularly the uniformity of surface. . . . If you look back at my paintings . . . the technique was always at a fairly pedestrian level and the uniformity was simply that of, say, monochromatic color rather than the way it was actually painted. They were never "well painted" by any standards. . . . as far as loose, painterly painting goes or the geometrical or hard-edge painting. . . . but I do think that a good pictorial idea is worth more than a lot of manual dexterity. Not that I necessarily have either one of those—it's that I think that is the easiest way to look at painting. At least, that's the conclusion I've drawn from looking at the painting that I liked.[48]

Jill. (1959)
Enamel on canvas, 7'6'' x 6'6''

The many slight changes in the widths of Stella's black bands, or in the character of their edges, are accidental in that no one of them was planned or represented a conscious artistic decision as such. But while no single variation that followed from Stella's willfully naïve technique has meaning in itself, the cumulative effect was an essential artistic decision and played a role of great importance in the ultimate expressiveness of the work. This may be likened to much of the local patterning in a Pollockian web, where the pouring and spattering allow for the occurrence of less than wholly determined markings. "These variations are absolutely a necessary part of my pictures," says Stella, "and represent a kind of rhythm: the way they were made."

The bands of the later Black paintings, those of the winter of 1959/60, tend to run parallel to the diagonal axes of the pictures' fields. In the simplest of these compositions, such as *Jill* (page 33), ten bands track in concentric patterns around the small diamond in the center, and the remaining four corners of the field are filled with bands paralleling those of the diamond. These latter might be considered segments of still larger concentric diamonds that would be completed only beyond the framing edge. In *Tuxedo Park* (page 38) two such diamonds are stacked vertically, while in *Gezira* (page 43), a painting of the same vertical format, one is centered between two half-diamonds. The diagonal tracking of the bands of these pictures involved turns which for the first time failed to reiterate the 90° angles of the corners of the field. This—combined with the sense of their completion beyond the frame—accounted for a less immediate relation of the patterns to the rectangular shape of the canvas. In drawings Stella made shortly afterward the trackings were even more complex. The unequivocal relationship of motif and field was only recaptured by Stella's decision to make the latter conform to the patterns he had drawn (as opposed to making the patterns conform to the shape of the field). This step led directly to the Aluminum series, Stella's first shaped canvases.

The emblematic patterns of the Black pictures were roughly sketched on yellow paper. These patterns as such are neither unique to Stella's work nor are they in themselves the substance of his paintings. The expressiveness of the paintings lies as much in everything else, that is, in how the patterns were used in the paintings—the size, the scale (the widths of the bands and interstices in relation to the size of the field and depth of the stretcher), the facture, and the paint quality. "A diagram is not a painting; it's as simple as that," Stella observed in the interview with Bruce Glaser. "I can make a painting from a diagram, but can you?"[49]

The relationship of the sketches to these early paintings is a clear but distant one. For Stella, the drawing always implies aspects of the painting of which only

Point of Pines. (1959)
Enamel on canvas, 7'3¾" x 9'1¼"

34

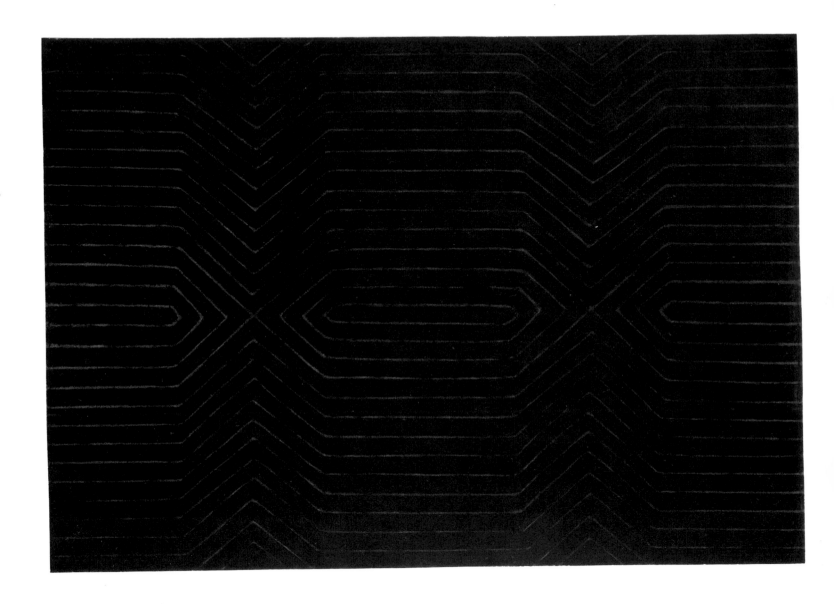

he is aware. But the making of the painting itself has the feeling of a wholly independent activity. "In other words," he has explained,

I wasn't translating an idea. When I'm painting the picture, I'm really painting a picture. I may have a flat-footed technique, or something like that, but still, to me, the thrill, or the meat of the thing, is the actual painting. I don't get any thrill out of laying it out. . . . I like the painting part, even when it's difficult. It's that *which seems most worthwhile to address myself to.*

One quality the configuration takes on in its conversion into painting is what Stella has referred to as "presence." This is a difficult word to define; it is ambivalently used, and much abused, in criticism. It refers to the way in which the work of art imposes itself on the perception and experience of the viewer. Though vague, it has been used even in so-called formalist criticism. Michael Fried, for example, author of some of the finest criticism on Stella, speaks of the "density of vital presence" in Stella's work.[50] Presence would seem, in the first instance, to be a function of size, but Clement Greenberg has observed— albeit in regard to sculpture—that "presence as achieved through size [is] aesthetically extraneous."[51] Indeed, we know that a small picture may have "presence," and a large picture lack it. I should like to define presence in painting as *the ability of a configuration to command its own space.* A small picture that lacks it seems trivial; a large picture, rhetorical.

But the factor of size does play a role in the aesthetic totality of the work. Greenberg himself has observed, in regard to color-field painting, that "size guarantees the purity as well as the intensity needed to suggest indeterminate space: more blue simply being bluer than less blue."[52] I have observed else- where that absolute size seems to have a meaning for a color painter such as Rothko that it did not for a fundamentally light-dark painter such as Pollock.[53] And although Stella's earlier pictures have nothing to do with color-field painting as such, large size plays an organic role in their conception which is as impor- tant—if not more so—as the role of size in color painting. In fact, as Stella himself has observed, his small paintings (as distinguished from drawings) rarely suc- ceed (as do those of Noland, for example).

The large size of Stella's painting from the time of the Black series onward appears to be necessary to the structure and meaning of the works. This is not simply a matter of scale relationships but of absolute size, and perhaps relates to the architectonic character of the pictures and their affinities to archi- tecture (see below, pp. 45, 129–31). It seems to apply most markedly in the most radically shaped pictures (see Stella's remarks, p. 68), which makes them look even more unsatisfactory in reproduction than is generally the case with large

abstract paintings. There exist, for example, small (ca. 2½ feet) versions of the pictures of the Copper series. These are not studies or maquettes for the large pictures but exact replicas in small size and were executed as an experiment after the larger pictures had been completed. Stella considers these pictures failures, and he is right. "Aside from sketches, all my pictures are fairly large," he has observed. "I don't think I've made a passable picture in the sort of 3-foot range and rarely attempted it. Those few times I have, it's been a kind of disaster."

Associated with this large size, which was standard for Stella from the outset, was a new sense of scale—a term I distinguish from simple size as having to do with the relationship of parts. This quality manifested itself when Stella's pictures were exhibited with Abstract Expressionist paintings of comparable size. They did not hang together comfortably and this was due less to differences in image or facture than to the wrenching dissimilarity in scale. A comparable dissimilarity also existed between Abstract Expressionism and the work of Kenneth Noland, Al Held, and others, suggesting that at the end of the fifties, a post-Abstract Expressionist scale was emerging. Stella sees this difference as stemming from the kind of organization he used. "Spanning the entire surface produces an effect of change of scale—the painting is more on the surface, there is less depth. And the picture seems bigger because it doesn't recede in certain ways or fade at the edge."

But the new scale was equally a matter of suppressing very small units. Large Abstract Expressionist pictures contain numerous very small markings or local changes of color and value which are played off against the dimensions of the larger compositional units and the size of the canvas itself. Stella's smallest *painted* unit is the width of the bands (ca. 2½ inches), which were laid down with a house painter's brush of that size. (The unpainted spaces between the bands are, to be sure, much narrower, but even if one reads them positively, they become lines that define 2½-inch planes.) This standardized band width established the modular unit. The serial hierarchies, therefore, were exhibited purely in terms of the lengths of the bands, which cumulatively established the largest unit of the painting—the over-all field. Though the concentric circular bands in Noland's paintings of the same period did vary somewhat in size, the narrowest was almost always at least a few inches in width, which created—as a minimal unit of measurement set against the size of the field—a comparable sense of breadth. "The development of a more accurate consciousness of the size and scale of both fields and their interior units," Stella considers,

combined with an awareness of the possibilities of modular repetition let me and, I believe, Ken Noland make more extreme paintings, in the sense of larger and shaped fields. Certain of the Abstract Expressionists had painted very big canvases but they were limited to rectangles. These pictures had considerable size but never the expanded or extended size and scale that would accommodate a sense of direction, speed, and vectored force.

THE SHIFT IN SIZE and scale from the work of the "first generation" artists to that of Stella and some of his contemporaries reflected, to some extent, a change in posture—the adoption of a more neutral, a less personal and Romantic form of address. The wall-size picture introduced by certain Abstract Expressionists around 1950 represented a crucial contribution to the vocabulary of modern painting, but that contribution lay elsewhere than in the simple fact of size. Even discounting architectural murals, such as those of the Mexicans, various precedents for sheer size existed in the works of Monet, Matisse, Picasso, Miró, Matta, and others. Rather, the giant American painting (rarer in the work of Pollock and other painters of his generation than is commonly supposed) distinguished itself by the projection into wall size—for the first time in the history of art—of an intimate and personal style containing no scale referent to the world of extra-pictorial objects. Giant pictures had previously been public in content, in manner, and in intended context. When Rothko said he painted large to be intimate, he was expressing a very special and new concept: the idea that a large abstract picture hanging in a private space, like that of an apartment, forces a new kind of contact between the painting and the viewer. The latter was perforce thrust close to Rothko's intimately nuanced surfaces.

The large Abstract Expressionist picture was neither a mural nor an easel picture but a hybrid which attained the size of the former while retaining the character of the latter. Instead of decorating the wall—as does the true architectural mural—it displaced it. The monumental art of the past, including large panel or easel pictures painted for palaces, was a public art. The large works of painters such as Pollock, Rothko, Newman, and Still were essentially private. They were intended for the private home rather than the public building, gallery, or museum. To some extent, this reflected the fact that during their pioneering years the Abstract Expressionists had no public. They were almost entirely ignored by the museums, and the galleries that championed them found precious few buyers for their work. Their "public"—aside from each other—consisted almost entirely of friends, or people associated with avant-garde circles: these were the *amateurs* (in the French sense of the word) who formed their audience.

The traumas resulting from this condition precipitated among the Abstract Expressionist artists an extreme distrust of the public situation. "It is . . . a risky act," Rothko warned, "to send [a picture] out into the world."[54] The scene that confronted the young artists emerging in the late fifties was very different. During those ten years a real audience outside the painters' own circle had emerged. This did not mean that the most challenging new work was taken up immediately. On the contrary, Stella, for example, sold very few pictures and received only rare favorable mentions in the press—amid a barrage of disparagement—during the first five years he exhibited. But it had become more a matter of time. By 1958, when Stella came to New York, the art-buying public had become convinced that Americans could produce major painting, worthy of comparison with the best of earlier European modern art. And it was now clear that this work could be sold at prices that made an artist's profession economically feasible.

The less painterly, bold, and flat large pictures of Stella and other abstract painters of his generation do not demand the intimate contemplation that Abstract Expressionist pictures want; they have a public as well as private face (unlike most Minimal sculpture, the very size of which determines its exclusively public address). "My pictures," says Stella,

are perfectly capable of functioning on a very public level—in a museum, an architectural setting, or something comparable. They have the scale and the brashness—or whatever it is—to carry that. But they also change. Put in more intimate surroundings, I think they are authentically and honestly adaptable to those kinds of situations. . . . We have a somewhat more neutral attitude [than the Abstract Expressionists], a more neutral way of addressing ourselves to painting.

This neutral form of address is also evident in the language and tone with which Stella and other younger painters are apt to speak about painting. By and large the Abstract Expressionists used a poetic language which more than occasionally bordered on the apocalyptic. Some of the most abstract of them—Newman and Still, for example—abhorred the language of formal criticism, a language Stella uses with a flat, disarming matter-of-factness. He thinks and speaks more in terms of plastic "problem-solving" than of "expression" and, on the face of it, would seem to be uninterested in the associational aspects of the image. "I always get into arguments," he has reported,

with people who want to retain the "old values" in painting—the "humanistic" values that they always find on the canvas. If you pin them down, they always end up asserting that there is something there besides the paint on the canvas. My painting is based on the fact that only what can be seen there is there. . . . If the painting were lean enough, accurate enough or right enough, you would just be able to look at it. All I want anyone to get out of my paintings, and all I ever get out of them, is the fact that you can see the whole idea without any confusion. . . . What you see is what you see.[55]

Gezira. (1960)
Enamel on canvas,
10'2" x 6'1"

This is not meant to imply, however, that painting is not meant to elicit an emotional response; that aspect is assumed in advance.

It does matter that for a painting to be successful, it has to deal with problems that are always given to painting, meaning the problems of what it takes to make a really good or convincing painting. But the worthwhile qualities of painting are always going to be both visual and emotional, and it's got to be a convincing emotional experience. Otherwise it will not be a good—not to say, great—painting.

Stella's style, and his attitude toward painting, to the extent that they were shared by his coevals, made applicable to them the term "cool generation." Insofar as this suggests a more consciously controlled, less improvisational art and a less Romantic, less passionate posture than that of the Abstract Expressionists, the term is not inaccurate. But despite their neutral form of address, these painters can—and do—feel equally passionate about painting. They may paint less volatile emotions, but they paint them with equal conviction.

To maintain Stella's own attitude in the discussion of his work would mean remaining almost entirely within the framework of formal criticism. The critic or art historian need not, of course, restrict himself to this language in discussing Stella, and it seems to me that such a restriction is especially limiting in regard to Stella's pre-1960 painting, for his Black pictures—and the attitude that informed them—differ from his later series in their somewhat more subjective, and more enigmatic, character. This resulted in part from the uneven reflectiveness of the black enamel (which soaked more completely into the cotton duck in some places than in others), and to the slight spreading of the enamel at the edges of the bands which partially obscure the unpainted interstitial strips, giving them a fugitive appearance. Late in 1959, I wrote of being "almost mesmerized by their [the Black pictures] eerie, magical presence."[56] Despite the somewhat different turn Stella's art was soon to take, and the different context in which we now see the Black pictures, I am not disposed to withdraw my words. By "mesmerized" I wanted to suggest something of the hypnotic regularity of the patterns (though this was not, by any means, comparable to the retinal tricks of so-called Op Art, which were yet to come). That the "presence" of the pictures seemed to me "eerie," had something to do with the strangeness and bleakness of Stella's black which, instead of absorbing the light, seemed irregularly to refract

it, the enamel having formed a film of uneven density on the surface. The association to "magic" had to do with the emblematic character of the pictures. There seemed to be something in them akin to prehistoric and primitive ritual art.

The general sense of Stella's Black paintings as enigmatic was not uncommon among the small group that received his art with approbation. Alfred Barr, one of the earliest of his champions, had seen these pictures in the summer of 1959. The following year he wrote of being "baffled" by the paintings but being "deeply impressed by their conviction." "I found my eye, as it were, spellbound, held by a mystery," he continued. "The term 'perseveration' seems superficially pertinent, yet the compulsiveness is controlled. To me the paintings express a stubborn, disciplined, even heroic rejection of worldly values."[57] In his recent discussion of these paintings Robert Rosenblum, who met Stella while teaching at Princeton, has observed that the "ubiquitous blackness" of these pictures "can evoke a mood of somber mystery; it is also a matter of the iconic structure, whose binary, cruciform, or concentric symmetries create an unworldly, hypnotic fixity, as of immutable, venerated emblems."[58]

Though Stella admits to the special character of the Black series, he feels that in the striped paintings as a whole there "aren't any particularly poetic or mysterious qualities," and he prefers to ascribe their enigmatic effects to "technical, spatial, and painterly ambiguities . . . [which produce] emotional ambiguities in the looking at the paintings."

To some extent, however, Stella's deadpan approach to the discussion of his painting is belied by the evidence of his own associations with them, as indicated by their titles. Whereas many non-figurative painters choose titles simply to avoid the confusion caused by identifying pictures by numbers, Stella invests considerable interest in his titles, which sometimes bear a rather direct associational relation to the image. *"Die Fahne hoch"*—The Flag on High—like other titles of the Black pictures, has a simple emotional straightforwardness that is akin to its emblematic mode. "The title" says Stella, "seems to me the way the painting looks, to say something about it. The feeling of the painting seems to me to have that kind of quality to it—Flags on high!—or something like that. . . . The thing that stuck in my mind was the Nazi newsreels—that big draped swastika—the big hanging flag—has pretty much those proportions."[59]

As in Stella's other series, there is an underlying unity among the titles of the Black pictures, though these titles were not arrived at as systematically as later ones were. The earlier, rectilinear Black pictures bear titles reflecting what Stella calls "downbeat" or "depressed political" situations. "Tomlinson Court Park," for example, refers to the Bedford-Stuyvesant area. "Arundel Castle" is the name of an apartment house near Tomlinson Court Park. The titles of the subsequent diamond-patterned Black pictures, such as *Zambesi* and *Club Onyx,* relate to the ambiance of black and deviate nightclubs. *Jill,* named after a young lady, might seem to be an exception among these Black pictures, but then, ''Jill was involved with some of those places.'' Stella's titles constitute personal associations with the pictures, and he would be horrified at the idea that a viewer might use them as a springboard to content. But the very fact of their existence—quite apart from the particular nature of the metaphors involved—suggests the way in which Stella is drawn to associations whose ambiguities potentially subvert the formal and intellectual rigor of his art.

Among the titles of the early paintings are a group that refer to buildings and locales, e.g., *Clinton Plaza, Arundel Castle, Reichstag, Getty Tomb, Astoria, Coney Island.* These foreshadow most of the titles of the later pictures which have been drawn from cities and towns as scattered in location as the San Juan Mountains of Colorado (the Copper series of 1960–61), Morocco (the square Day-Glo pictures of 1964–65), New Hampshire (the Irregular Polygons of 1966), and Asia Minor (the Protractor series begun in 1967). While these titles—along with those taken from British clipper ships (the Notched V series of 1964–65)— reflect the painter's peripatetic tastes, they even more importantly express his abiding interest in architecture.

Stella's affinity tor architecture relates in the first instance to the architectonic character of his enterprise as a painter. Not surprisingly, ever since his student days he had admired the architecture of the Chicago School and the International Style. (Interestingly enough, he discovered at one point that motifs he had employed independently had earlier been used by Frank Lloyd Wright as architectural decoration.) The title of the painting *Reichstag* alludes to the planning of Nazi Berlin, which aroused his curiosity, as did Mussolini's constructions in Rome.[60] And though the classicism of Fascist architecture was academic while that of the International Style was intrinsic, they were two sides of the same coin in their commitment to the underlying symmetry of the classical aesthetic. ''The idea of symmetry was in disrepute among painters,'' Stella has observed, ''but it seemed to me that it could be used.''

By its very nature, architecture potentially exerts a kind of control and authority over the spectator's experience, which not only Stella but other painters of large-size abstract painting since World War II have sought—consciously or unconsciously—to attain. The size of the traditional easel picture, which functions as a window on another world, gives the spectator the option of simply disregarding it if he chooses. The large picture, which displaces or identifies itself with the wall, imposes itself on the spectator in a more authoritative way, in the manner of architecture itself. Nor is this control a function only of particular modes of modern architecture. Fascist architecture aspired to sheer domination more conspicuously than other modes. Yet, by its very lack of inventiveness, that architecture did not control the spectator's experience, nor characterize his environment, with anything like the authority exercised by Wright or Mies van der Rohe, especially in their public buildings. As a painter, Stella is very aware of wanting to achieve "some of the control that any architectural situation normally imposes."[61]

The size of Stella's pictures is the primary factor in determining the quasi-architectural role they play. In addition, the lateral and recessional space of his paintings is very tightly controlled. "You have a limited access, and in that sense it is more like a building than an illusion of limitless space." Stella saw the architectonic patterns of the Black paintings as a "bleak beginning which would actually give me something to build on." "They're architectonic," he observes,

in the sense of building—of making buildings. My whole way of thinking about painting has a lot to do with building—having foundations to build on. The Black pictures were a groundwork structure in more ways than one. I enjoy and find it more fruitful to think about many organizational or spatial concepts in architectural terms, because when you think about them strictly in design terms, they become flat and very boring problems. So I guess I use a little bit of the outside world by bringing in architecture as another way of looking at the problems, as a way of expanding them. But I think my painting remains a distinctly pictorial experience—it's not finally an architectural one. It doesn't really need to have anything to do with architecture, or the [spectator's] ability to understand architecture.

Not surprisingly for an artist with these proclivities, Stella has occasionally explored some purely architectural ideas. He made preliminary studies for the design of an art gallery at the suggestion of the dealer Ileana Sonnabend; another set of designs, for an "ideal museum," included a variable wall arrangement that functioned in tandem with a floor that could be raised and lowered—the entire system suspended and standing free within a glass cage. More immediately related to his painting was a proposal for a ceiling in the Long Island home of a private collector. This amounted to a form of architectural relief sculpture based upon the pattern of the mitered maze pictures of 1961–63 (see below, pp. 75–76). The ceiling was to have descended about 2 feet, in 1-inch steps at each turn of the maze. And the plaster was to be polychromed in a sequential manner related to the left-hand section of *Jasper's Dilemma* (page 77).

Frank Stella, New York, 1959

BEFORE STELLA HAD completed his last Black paintings he began a series of sketches for new works in which the individual bands were intended to function more autonomously in relation to the heraldic pattern as a whole. These sketches became the basis of the Aluminum paintings, Stella's first shaped canvases. The particular character of this group came, he recalls, from

thinking more about the individual units of the pattern—the bands. They are about the "traveling" of the bands. In other words, a band moves along, jogs to the side, and turns again to resume its original direction. That makes up a given unit: a band with a jog in it. And then everything is worked out to make that consistent . . . *The bands in the Black pictures weren't meant to "travel" that much—those pictures were more a pattern imposed on a field. The units in the Aluminum pictures were intended to be more individual, put together to make something like a "force field" (to use the term Carl Andre was fond of).*

The consistency that Stella mentions in this passage was not, however, present in his first sketches for the Aluminum paintings. As each band followed another—with each successive "jog" occurring one modular unit farther down the face of the canvas—serial patterns were created which, when fitted into the rectangular field of the picture, "had spaces left over in them."[62] For example, the pattern of *Kingsbury Run* (page 51) was originally placed within such a regular field, and two small squares in the upper left- and lower right-hand corners of the painting thus constituted "leftovers." These areas lacked design con-

Avicenna. (1960)
Aluminum paint on canvas,
6' x 6'

View of exhibition at Leo Castelli Gallery, New York, September–October 1960

sistency insofar as they did not function as integral parts of the jogging band pattern. Of course, a similar inconsistency could be ascribed to segments in the patterns of the Black pictures (those bands without right-angle turns in the four corners of *"Die Fahne hoch,"* for example). But in the Black pictures, the greater primacy of the pattern as a single cohesive entity and—at least in the later examples with diamond motifs—the looser relationship of the pattern to the architecture of the framing edge, seemed to minimize this inconsistency as an issue. Moreover, the Black pictures were, on every level of their conception and execution, somewhat less rigorous and less consciously wrought than all of Stella's subsequent stripe pictures.

The problem, then, was how to achieve an absolute serial consistency with the bands. Stella was uneasy about his first sketches for the Aluminum paintings. He liked what he had achieved in the traveling of the bands but was dissatisfied with the leftover boxes. While visiting Princeton one day, he showed Darby Bannard the sketches and complained about the leftover spaces. Bannard suggested the possibility of simply cutting the boxes out. "I thought about it

for a little while," Stella recalls, "and said: 'Well, that's obviously the thing to do. If you don't want it, take it away.' So I just began to build the stretchers leaving out the part I didn't want. And once I started with the Aluminum paintings, they naturally kept suggesting more and more possibilities for shaped pictures."[63]

As the pioneer of the "shaped canvas," Stella opened a series of possibilities explored by other painters—and some sculptors—in the middle 1960s. But we must keep in mind that we are speaking here of only a special kind of shaped canvas. Canvases—or other picture supports—that depart from the traditional rectangle or tondo form are not without precedent in modern painting, and they were used at least as early as the second decade of this century. De Chirico, for example, worked with triangles, trapezoids, and (at least once) an irregular polygon; Arp used biomorphic supports. But in their work, and in that of other artists who experimented with shaped fields, the picture (or configuration) was painted *inside* the preconceived shaped frame and was only elliptically related to it. In Stella, the irregular shape of the field was a function of the pattern governing it, and their identities were inseparable.

Stella was the first to succeed in keeping an abstract picture on an irregular field from taking on the appearance of flat relief sculpture. (In de Chirico, any such tendency was overcome by his reliance on illusionistic imagery and space —a reliance that drained visual importance away from the framing edge.) In Arp, where the surface was unmodeled and abstract, the edge dominated and turned the work essentially into a form of sculptural relief. The same tendencies are visible in the paintings of other artists, such as Riva Urban and Sven Lukin, who explored shaped fields in the late fifties and sixties. Stella's solution to the problem lay in his *identification* of the field-shape with that of the pattern of the surface. Seen as the edge of that pattern, the shape of the irregular picture support was deprived of the autonomy—the separate identity—possessed by the outer contour of earlier shaped picture supports or reliefs.

The new emphasis given the shape of the field in the Aluminum paintings follows from a basic difference between their patterns and those of the Black pictures. In the latter the pattern is usually biaxially symmetrical and thus extendable by continuing the pattern on all four sides from the center of the picture. In the Aluminum series the center of the field is not—except in *Avicenna* (page 49) and *Averroes*[64]—the focal point of the pattern; it is not even readily discovered in most examples. Their symmetry is no longer biaxial. (In *Kingsbury Run* it is only diagonal.) The principle of extension in these pictures is additive rather than radial. The vertical tracks are added together so that the outer edges of the first and last literally constitute the flanking limits of the picture support.

Kingsbury Run. (1960) Aluminum paint on canvas, 6'6'' x 6'6''

50

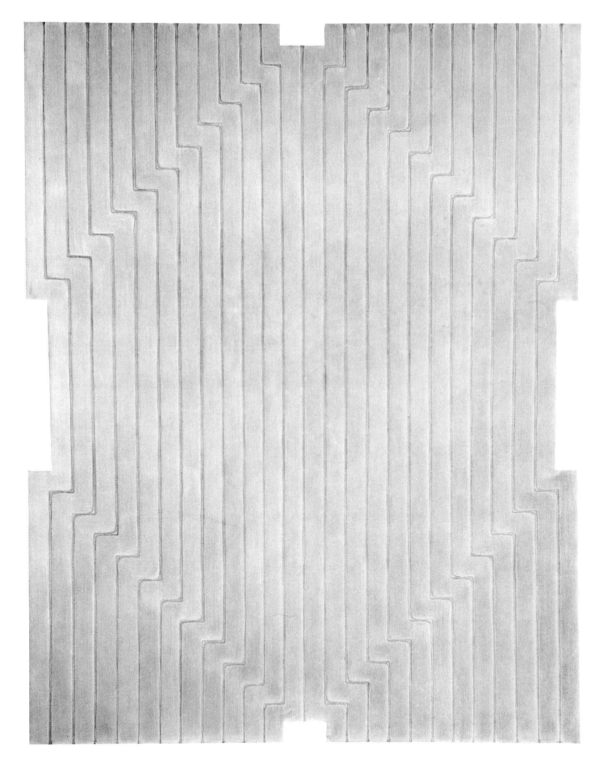

Marquis de Portago. (1960)
Aluminum paint on canvas,
7'9" x 5'11¼"

Though the notches in the Aluminum pictures represent only a small departure from the rectangle when compared with Stella's subsequent more radical shaping, they constitute the beginning of this main line in his development. By moving drawing to the boundaries of the picture field he would increasingly attribute new importance to shape—an element that had virtually disappeared from much of the avant-garde painting of the late forties and fifties. Shape—in any traditional or conventional sense of the term—played no important role in Pollock's classic style, or in the work of Newman or Rothko. In Pollock's new form of "contourless" drawing, for example, line did not enclose or define shape. Nor did the "zips," bands, or color-field divisions that traversed the surfaces of Newman's paintings cut out shapes; and the rectangles of Rothko, precisely because they functioned mainly as echoes of the framing edge, constituted a rejection of deliberate shaping on the artist's part. Stella's work provides in this regard a strong contrast to that of Pollock, Newman, and Rothko. Michael Fried, in his essay on Stella's 1966 pictures, would clearly have included the artist's entire development starting with the Aluminum pictures when he observed that they "investigate the viability of shape as such," by which "I mean its power to hold, to stamp itself out, and *in*—as verisimilitude and narrative and symbolism used to impress themselves—compelling conviction. Stella's undertaking in these paintings is therapeutic: to restore shape to health . . ."[65]

That the new shaping would take place at the picture's edge, that it would be *of* the field of the canvas as much as *in* it, was to some extent foreshadowed in the work of Newman. The configurations of Pollock and Rothko were positioned inside the edge of the picture field, and they worked to define a space that was in a limited sense still illusionistic. Newman's pictures, on the other hand, especially those of less painterly execution, were more unequivocally flat. Their only articulation consisted of bands reaching from one end of the field to the other. These exactly paralleled two sides of the framing edge and locked themselves at right angles between the other two. With the surface planes appearing neither behind nor in front of the framing edge, the latter lost the final vestige of its role as "window" and appeared virtually in the state it possessed before the surface was painted—that is, as the first four "lines" of the painting.

But the emphasis that Newman gave to the size and shape of the picture field was also achieved negatively, by his extreme reduction of visual "incident" within the field. Thus, a canvas might have only a single vertical (or horizontal) line, or planar division, over its entire (often very large) surface. With the size and shape of the canvas playing such an important role in the visual experience, it was natural that Newman should explore the expressive possibilities of unfamiliar formats, though until recently he never departed from the rectangle. Indeed, to the extent that the rectangle is as much a shape as any other form (though more regular, of course), the primary role given by Newman to formats of often unusual dimensions would almost seem to entitle him to the role of "father" of the shaped canvas.

In view of Newman's role in this regard, and of Stella's development, the question of the relationship between the two artists is critical. My own contention is that Newman's influence on Stella was at the most indirect, and insofar as it existed at all, it occurred after the establishment of the main premises of Stella's art. Others see a much more direct line of descent from Newman to Stella, and much of what has been written to this effect has been influenced by an extremely important, and closely argued text on Stella written by Michael Fried in 1965.[66] A central aspect of his analysis of Stella's stripe paintings hinges upon Fried's theory of "deductive structure." I wish to take exception to this theory as it relates to Stella for two important reasons. First, it posits a relationship between Newman and Stella which is misleading; second, by omitting the crucial influence of Jasper Johns, it gives a somewhat unbalanced picture of recent art history. Given the nature of Fried's thinking (which, among critics, most closely approximates Stella's own), the conviction of his writing, and its influence, a resumé and discussion of his theory is necessary.

In his text Fried first expounded his theory of "deductive structure" and described Newman as the pioneer in this area. The bands, or "zips" in Newman's paintings

provide a crucial element of pictorial structure, by means of what I want to term their "deductive" relation to the framing-edge. That is, the bands amount to echoes within the painting of the two side framing-edges; they relate primarily to these edges, and in so doing make explicit acknowledgment of the shape of the canvas. They demand to be seen as deriving from the framing-edge—as having been "deduced" from it—though their exact placement within the colored field has been determined by the painter, with regard to coloristic effect rather than to relations that could be termed geometrical. Newman's pioneering exploration of "deductive" pictorial structure represents an important new development in the evolution of one of the chief preoccupations of modernist painting from Manet through Synthetic Cubism and Matisse: namely, the increasingly explicit recognition of the physical characteristics of the picture-support.[67]

Both Stella and Noland are seen as having drawn implications from this approach.

Like Newman and Noland, Stella is concerned with deriving or deducing pictorial structure from the literal character of the picture-support; but his work differs from theirs in its exaltation of deductive structure as sufficient in itself to provide the substance, and not just the scaffolding or syntax, of major art. . . . [The] first black paintings . . . amounted to the most extreme statement yet made advocating the importance of the literal character of the picture-support for the determination of pictorial structure. . . . In subsequent series of paintings executed in aluminum, copper and magenta metallic paint . . . Stella's grasp of deductive structure grew more and more tough-minded: until the paintings came to be generated in toto, as it were, by the different shapes of the framing edge . . .[68]

The implication of the theory, simply stated, is that the character and shape of the picture support came first, the internal structure second. But, although Fried specifically asserts the primacy *of* the shape of the field over the patterning *on* the field—the latter being deduced from the former—he also sees a subtle and complex interplay between the two:

. . . there is . . . an important sense in which Stella's ambition to make paintings whose stripe-patterns appear to be generated by the different shapes of the picture-support exerted strong influence upon the character of the shapes themselves. That is, although the shapes appear to generate the stripe-patterns, the prior *decision to achieve deductive structure by means of this particular relation between the stripes and the framing-edge played an important role in determining the character of the shapes.[69]*

Fried's analysis of Stella's art was further elaborated in an essay on Stella's 1966 pictures published a year later.[70] Writing specifically of the Aluminum pictures, Fried asserted that their

stripes begin at the framing-edge and reiterate the shape of that edge until the entire picture is filled; moreover, by actually shaping each picture . . . Stella was able to make the fact that the literal shape determines the structure of the entire painting completely perspicuous. That is, in each painting the stripes appear to have been generated by the framing-edge and, starting there, to have taken possession of the rest of the canvas, as though the whole painting self-evidently followed from, not merely the shape of the support, but its actual physical limits.[71]

Once again Fried modifies his assertion by describing the subtle interrelationship between the shape of the field and the pattern on it.

In both Noland's and Stella's (stripe) paintings the burden of acknowledging the shape of the support is borne by the depicted shape, or perhaps more accurately, by the relationship between it and the literal shape—a relation that declares the primacy of the latter. And in general the development of modernist painting during the past six years can be described as having involved the progressive assumption by literal shape of a greater—that is, more active, more explicit—importance than ever before, and the consequent subordination of depicted shape. It is as though depicted shape has become less and less capable of venturing on its own, of pursuing its own ends; as though unless, in a given painting, depicted shape manages to participate in—by helping to establish— the authority of the shape of the support, conviction is aborted and the painting fails. In this sense depicted shape may be said to have become dependent upon literal shape—and indeed unable to make itself felt as shape except by acknowledging that dependence.[72]

Within the various emphases of Fried's theory, there are two distinct levels of argument. On the first, he speaks of the way in which the paintings are conceived and attributes to Stella the actual process of deductive thought. (He speaks, for instance, of Stella's "*prior* decision to achieve deductive structure.") On the second level, he is concerned to describe the effect of the finished pictures themselves, irrespective of the genesis of the conception. That is, he speaks of the stripes as *appearing* to have been "generated by the framing-edge and, starting there, to have taken possession of the rest of the canvas, *as though* the whole painting self-evidently followed from . . . the shape of the support."[73] In the essay of the previous year he had spoken of "Stella's ambition to make paintings whose stripe-patterns *appear* to be generated by the different shapes of the picture-support . . ."[74] What Fried is concerned about on this second level of his argument is the effect that the picture creates—how it actually seems to him to work.

While granting the subtleties and complexities of Fried's presentation of deductive structure, I find it impossible to subscribe to its basic premises—as they relate to Stella—or to the implications that follow from them. The principal tenet of the theory asserts the primacy *of* the shape of the field, or picture support, over the patterning *on* the field, which is seen as subsequently "deduced" from that shape. Moreover, in insisting that the conception of the picture depends upon the primacy of the edge, it implies that the picture asks to be read from the framing edge inward. In a great many of the stripe paintings (especially in the Black series), however, the strongest optical effect is quite the opposite; the patterns and lines radiate out from the center of the canvas toward the edge, and although the role played by the center of the canvas makes "explicit acknowledgment of the shape of the canvas," it does not seem possible to interpret the motifs as having been simply deduced from that shape. (Stella,

Newstead Abbey. (1960) Aluminum paint on canvas, 10' x 6'

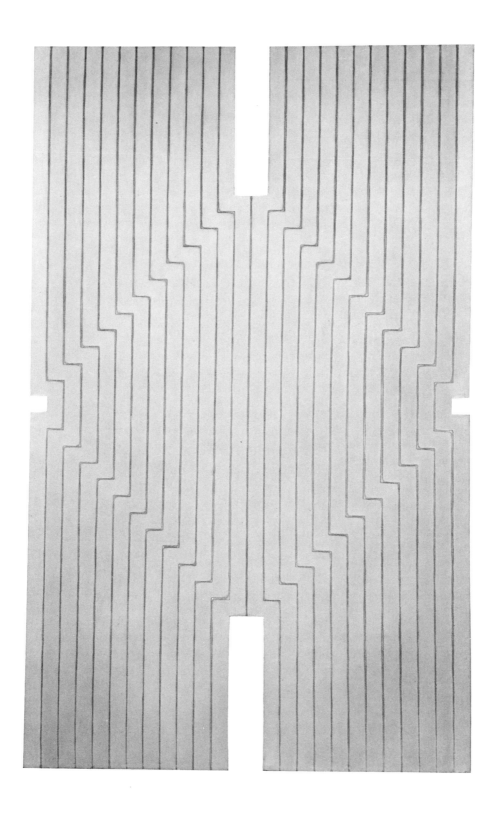

as we have seen, thinks of the Black pictures as "more a pattern imposed on a field.")

In the Aluminum pictures the strongest optical movement—the surface "ripple" that proceeds *diagonally* across the canvas (see below, p. 63)—results from the serial and additive nature of the composition rather than from the frame. The canvas shape here follows from the serial progression of the bands rather than being an a priori shape that generates them. This is strongly reinforced by our knowledge of how Stella actually arrived at these first shaped canvases; if the question of "primacy" is relevant at all in the case of the Aluminum pictures, the framing edge was, in fact, deduced from the surface pattern rather than vice versa (see above, p. 47).[75]

As Stella progressed beyond the Aluminum series, there was no question of deriving the surface pattern from the shape of the canvas (or vice versa). The two were conceived simultaneously; in their reciprocity, neither could be said to be "deduced" from the other. "It became completely reversible," Stella says. "They have to be that way because it's one kind of drawing. I don't think of the perimeter as such . . . when I see the outline of the picture I see the interior drawing with it. In other words, I see a line drawing of the idea. I never see just a cutout of the shape." While the very term "deduction" presupposes the primacy of one component over the other, the evidence presented by the paintings, especially those of the Aluminum series through 1965, is that there was no such primacy. The pictures ask to be read not from the framing edge inward, nor from the center outward, but in a single simultaneous perception of the total image. Whereas Fried does, within the context of the deductive framework, allow for the interdependence of the painted pattern and the framing edge and for the reciprocal power each exerts on the other, his assertion of the primacy of one of the components involved argues against this simultaneity of perception.

Unless one can accept deductive theory as applicable to Stella, one must naturally question Fried's thesis of the influence of Newman on Stella. In discussing the evolution of modernist pictorial structure, Fried ascribed the dominant influence to Pollock, Louis, and Newman. All three, he rightly claims, played an important role in altering the function of the picture support. But it was Newman, Fried continues, who placed a new kind of emphasis on pictorial structure based on the shape and size, rather than on the flatness, of the picture support. Fried states that as early as 1958–59 it was "partly in direct response to the work of Barnett Newman"[76] that Stella produced his first Black paintings. He sees the line of development moving from Newman directly to Stella's "exaltation" of the deductive process. Since Fried quite rightly sees the sparsely placed bands of Newman as deduced from the frame, the implication is that the multiple bands of Stella were arrived at by somehow applying Newman's deductive principle more vigorously. But Newman's bands function quite differently. Unlike Stella's they do not in themselves constitute the field; they differ from one another in width, texture, and degree of painterliness, and—above all—they are sparsely placed in the fields that they resonate and divide. The contiguous and repetitive bands in Stella's paintings collectively form a geometrical motif.

Indeed, Stella's original inspiration for the striping in the Black series, insofar as there was one, was not Newman but Jasper Johns. As we have seen, the repetitive stripes and bands of the latter's Flags in particular had made a considerable impression on Stella while he was still at Princeton (see above, p. 12). Moreover, it is in certain of those paintings by Johns that we see stated for the first time, albeit in figurative form, the absolute identification of the motif with the shape of the field; the simultaneous and reciprocal relationship between the picture edge as motif edge and as field boundary.[77] Stella first saw pictures by Johns in January 1958—several months before he left Princeton and began work on the Black series. He was well advanced into this series before he had ever seen the work of Newman, which he encountered for the first time in the French & Co. retrospective of March 1959. In defining Stella's role in the history of recent art, therefore, it is essential to stress the contribution made by Johns to the early formative phase of his development. While Stella's place in the over-all history of abstract painting in the fifties and sixties must be seen very much in relationship to that of Newman, with whom he feels a deep affinity in terms of broader aims, it would be a mistake to posit that Newman played any role in the formation of Stella's style.

[After this book was completed it was brought to my attention that a footnote in Fried's introduction to the catalogue of the Jules Olitski retrospective at the Corcoran Gallery in 1967 contained a repudiation of his own theory of deductive structure. In the text of this essay Fried observed: "Roughly, Noland and Stella became painters of major importance when they began to relate the elements within their paintings to the shape of the support in such a way that the structure of their paintings could be said to *acknowledge* that shape more lucidly and explicitly than had ever been the case."[77a] In the footnote appended to this sentence, we read:

The concept of acknowledgment is meant to displace the notion of "deductive structure," which I have used in the past to describe the structural mode of Noland's and Stella's paintings and which now seems to me inadequate. One trouble with that notion was that it could be taken to imply that any *structure in which elements are aligned with the framing-edge is as "deductive (more or less) as any other. Whereas by emphasizing the need to* acknowledge *the shape of the support I mean to call attention to the fact that what, in a given instance,* will count as *acknowledgment remains to be discovered, to be made out.*[77b]

Inasmuch as Fried's *Three American Painters* still stands, and very rightly so, as "one of the essential documents in any discussion of the esthetics of painting in the present decade,"[77c] and his "Shape as Form: Frank Stella's Recent Painting" remains crucial to the literature on Stella, it seems to me that the subsequent disavowal of deductive structure contained in the footnote cited above does not eliminate the need to confront an idea that has been widely accepted in critical writing and discussion. Moreover, the repudiation in question does not take up the substantive problems that follow from deductive structure, such as how Stella actually worked, the specific relationships of framing edge to surface motif in his shaped canvases, and the possible rapports between his work and that of Newman and Johns.]

During his first months in New York, Stella became intrigued with the metallic paints he saw on sample cards of commercial paint dealers but "didn't know what to do with them" at the time. It was while first sketching the designs for what would become the Aluminum series that he began to think about the possibilities of metallic paint. The black paint had still carried with it the implications of the chiaroscuro shading, and hence the space, of representational art. "The aluminum surface," Stella recalls,

had a quality of repelling the eye in the sense that you couldn't penetrate it very well. It was a kind of surface that wouldn't give in, and would have less soft, landscape-like or naturalistic space in it. I felt that it had the character of being slightly more abstract. But there was also a lot of ambiguity in it. It identifies as its own surface, yet it does have a slightly mysterious quality in one sense. You know it's on the surface, but it catches just enough light to have a shimmer. That shimmering surface has very much its own kind of surface illusionism, its own self-contained space. You can't quite go into it. And it holds itself in a nice way on the surface as far as painting problems are concerned.

The more abstract, less organic character of the aluminum paint followed also from the fact that metallic colors are not the colors one sees in nature. To the extent that they carry associations, these are associations to the world of man-made objects, particularly industrial products and machinery, with their

60

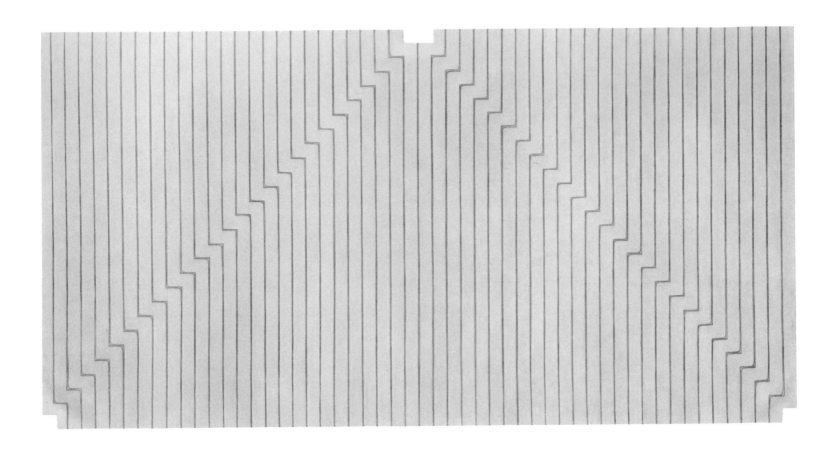

Union Pacific. (1960)
Aluminum paint on canvas,
6'5¼'' x 12'4½''

more regular geometrical forms and sharply defined edges. The aluminum paint, as opposed to the copper that Stella chose next, was also rather cool in tone.

Such "cool" and metallic qualities reflected the more consciously rigorous spirit that informed Stella's painting at this point and was also visible in small but important changes of execution. The paint film of the Black series had involved somewhat uneven densities in the layering and a soft, irregular edge. The bands of the Aluminum pictures were applied in a way that left far fewer traces of the artist's hand. The surface was more even and the edges were cut sharply "as with a sash tool" (a small angled brush which house painters use to cut around the molding of windows). This sharpness was somewhat modified, however, by a slight "bleeding" of the oily binding agent in the aluminum paint, a process that satisfied Stella's desire to "gray out" somewhat the unpainted strips. Finally, while the patterns of the Black pictures were laid out freehand, those of the Aluminum paintings were guided by ruled pencil lines, which are still visible on the surface in the unpainted interstices between the bands.

As total compositions, the Aluminum pictures declared their abstractness and flatness even more frankly than did the Black ones. But while the elusive and ubiquitous "soft" space of the latter had vanished, the successive jogs in the bands of the new pictures introduced the illusion of a very shallow, but tightly controlled ripple in the space. This illusion was strengthened by Stella's method of applying the paint: the brush followed the direction of the band, and at those points where it encountered a jog, it proceeded for a short space at right angles to the prevailing direction. The light reflected by the metallic particles at these points was thus of a slightly different value, and it had the effect of creating a series of depressions or ridges, depending on the angle of the light. Taken together, these constitute a continuing vector of movement across an otherwise static field. In this sense, they relate to Stella's description of the patterns in the Aluminum pictures as "something like a 'force field.'" We see them running from the lower left corner to the upper center and down again to the lower right corner in *Union Pacific* (page 62) and moving diagonally upward to (or downward from) the upper center of *Luis Miguel Dominguín* (page 61).

The titles of the Black pictures had tended toward the "depressed" or "downbeat." With a few exceptions, those of the Aluminum series "get sort of literary or glamorous—like Arabic philosophers, bullfighters, and racing drivers." A few suggest closer relationships with the configurations than do others. Stella associated the four corner shapes of *Marquis de Portago* (page 52) with the fenders of the racing car of the ill-fated Marquis, and the single long diagonal depression of *Kingsbury Run* (page 51) suggested to him the name of a ravine in Cleveland, site of a celebrated murder.

Ouray. (1960–61)
Copper paint on canvas,
7′9¾″ x 7′9¾″

View of exhibition at Leo Castelli Gallery, New York, April–May 1962

THE SIX LARGE Copper paintings of 1960–61,[78] named after towns in Colorado's San Juan Mountains, are the most radically shaped of Stella's pictures. In the Aluminum series, the shaping was limited to the removal of small notches or, at most, segments of bands (as in *Luis Miguel Dominguín*) from the perimeters of the rectangular fields. But the shapes of the Copper pictures only remotely implied such underlying rectangles. Unlike the profiles of the Aluminum pictures, their cutout perimeters involved considerable subtractions from the rectangular field and their silhouettes bore an optical emphasis at least equal to the accompanying surface patterns.

Closest in character to Stella's earlier designs was the biaxially symmetrical *Ouray* (page 65),[79] where large square areas were cut away from the four corners of a square field to produce the shape of a Greek cross. The surface of the reverse L-shaped *Creede* (page 66) involved a cutting away of four-ninths of the area of a square from which it might have been derived. Unlike the other Copper paintings, and—for that matter—all Stella's prior pictures, *Creede* departs entirely from the notion of a symmetrical design.

Ophir (page 69) is diagonally symmetrical, but its shape is the most radical of all the Copper pictures. Its horizontal segment is the only passage in these works which cannot be construed as deriving from the perimeter of an imaginary

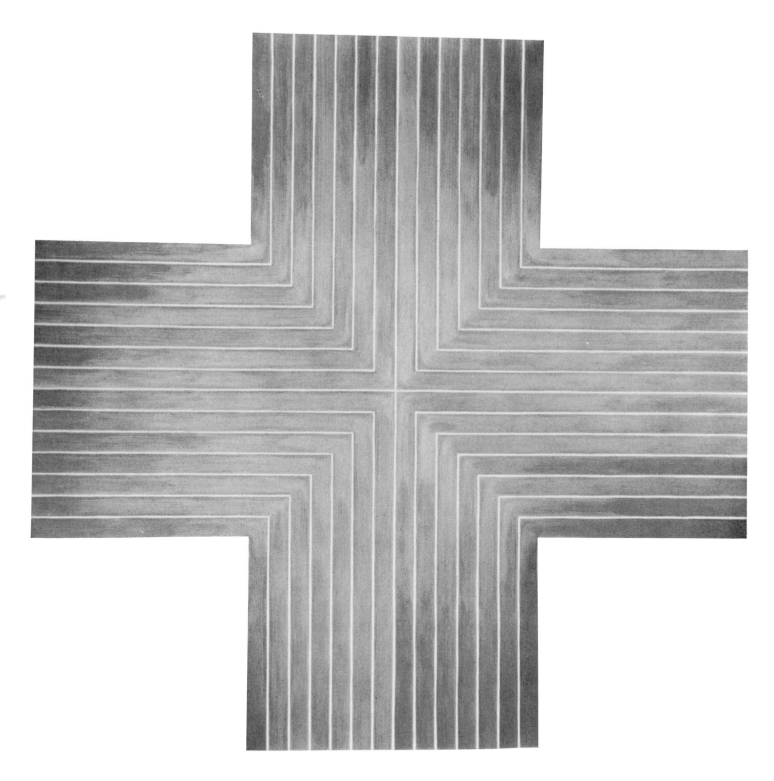

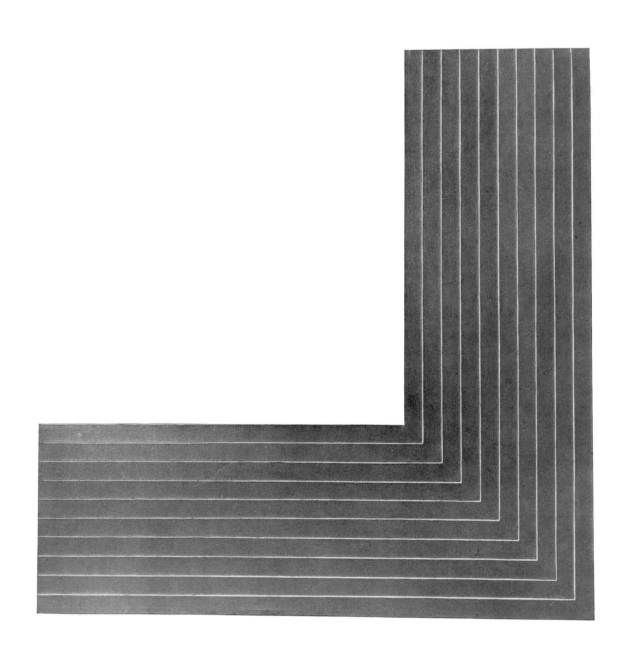

Creede I. (1961). Copper paint on canvas, 6'10½'' x 6'10½''

Lake City. (1960–61). Copper paint on canvas, 6′10½″ x 9′2¼″

square or rectangle. In that sense it seems to pick up, and carry to an extreme, the vector-like traveling of the bands characteristic of the Aluminum pictures, independently of the larger "force field" within which these had operated. In becoming, in effect, all vector, it anticipated the conception of the Running V series of 1964–65 (see below pp. 101–4). Since the distinguishing characteristic of *Ophir*'s shape was its greater independence from the rectangular norm that dominated Stella's other Copper paintings, it is not surprising that a good deal of ambiguity was created with regard to the location of *Ophir*'s visual center. "*Ophir* begins rather to have an up and down movement," Stella notes, "and creates some tension as to where the symmetrical relationships are. Locating the center of the picture seems to me the basic problem."

The shaping of the Copper pictures seemed to some observers at the time to carry Stella's new works out of the realm of painting into a form of sculptural relief. There is no doubt, of course, that these pictures did contain the seeds of certain possibilities subsequently explored by other artists in the form of freestanding Minimal and serial sculpture. But for Stella, one purpose of the Copper pictures was precisely to test the limits of the conventions of painting in regard to the shape of the field, and to do this in such a way that the resulting images would "hold" the wall as painting. "The Copper pictures were a big jump," Stella recalls,

and I was aware that they raised questions about relief and sculpture. But I knew where I stood, and wasn't afraid of the problem. . . . Although these are the most radically shaped of the canvases they are also the most rectilinear in a way. In other words, they emphasize the right angle, and what those right-angle turns do. But they represented the extreme—the limit—to which I could take the shaping. Even though so much is cut away—and in some cases, so arbitrarily—what saves them, I think, is the fact that they keep echoing a kind of rectilinearity. If they started getting off into different kinds of obtuse and acute angles, they would be lost as paintings.

The large size of the Copper paintings also played a role in offsetting visual problems raised by the marked shaping of the fields. Stella later painted a series of small (ca. 2½ feet) replicas of the larger Copper pictures, and the small size seemed incapable of carrying the shape. "The shaping was radical for them," Stella admits. "They became too plaque-like—like cutouts, or illustrations of cutouts."

It is not surprising that around the time he completed the Copper pictures Stella gave some thought to the making of sculpture, and it is worth noting that throughout the sixties he maintained close friendships with Carl Andre and

Ophir. (1960–61)
Copper paint on canvas,
8'2½'' x 6'10¾''

Donald Judd (for both of whose work he has a high regard). Among Stella's ideas was a project for sets of concentric squares that receded pyramidally, "like an inverted funnel," and came out again on the other side. But he finally rejected these ideas to concentrate exclusively on painting. "Most of them would have looked Minimal—and probably pretty horrible," Stella observed. "I like painting a lot. If I made sculpture, it would somehow be frivolous. It would be for fun, not out of necessity. Painting has everything I need. It provides a full range of possibility and involvement. Pictorial space seems to be quite adaptable, and quite expandable to whatever you want to do with it."

The development of what is collectively called Minimal sculpture varies from artist to artist and derives from a multiplicity of sources. But it was certainly generally influenced by Stella's geometrical profiles and serial relationships and by the work of other abstract painters who used simple heraldic formats. Some critics have seen it as evolving naturally from the "objectification" and shaping of paintings. But most Minimal sculpture strikes Stella as more a mistaken plastic "gesture" than a form of affective aesthetic expression. "It was to the detriment of sculpture," Stella asserts,

that it picked up the simplest things that were going on in painting. The sculptors just scanned the organization of painting and made sculpture out of it. It was a bad reading of painting; they really didn't get much of what the painting was about. Repetition is a problem, and I don't find it particularly successful in the form of sculptural objects. There are certain strong qualities in the pictorial convention—the way in which perimeter, area, and shape function—that allow a serial pattern to derive benefits from them. Repeated units on a unified painted ground function a lot differently than do separate units standing on the floor or nailed to the wall. Of course the sculptors will say that it's just a failure in the development of our ability to see—that we're not seeing their work right.

The program of much of this sculpture was, to be sure, based precisely on the notion that the conventions of which Stella speaks constituted the fatal limitation of painting. Misreading his enterprise, some sculptors saw his shaped canvases as pointing ineluctably to their three-dimensional art. To that extent, the historical position of Minimal sculpture is more that of a tangential offshoot of late-fifties abstract painting than it is a continuation of the main line of sculptural development that passed through David Smith.

THE COPPER SERIES was followed in 1961 by a group of six square (77 x 77") pictures shown at the Galerie Lawrence, Paris, and never exhibited in the United States. These occupy a special position in Stella's development in that they

Island No. 10. (1961)
Alkyd on canvas,
6'5" x 6'5"

70

72

contain the root vocabulary of all that had gone before. It was as if he had worked his way back to the primary form of the patterns of which the Black and Copper pictures might be considered derivations. In their extreme simplicity, and the absolute evenness of their matte surface, these pictures have a kind of immediacy that was not to be found in the more complex structures, the more elusive and ambiguous light, and the more painterly execution—relatively speaking—of the Black, Aluminum, and Copper pictures. "Those six simple designs, painted in Benjamin Moore flat wall paint, were really all the things the earlier pictures weren't," Stella observes. "They were very symmetrical, very flat and very all-over. They might not have been such successful pictures, and afterward, I turned away from that kind of thing. But they were certainly the clearest statement to me, or to anyone else, as to what my pictures were about—what kind of goal they had. I think getting close to that goal turned me to something else."

In focusing upon the square, Stella was insisting on the simplest and most regular of all rectilinear formats and the one which, by implication, had provided the underpinning of the radically shaped Copper pictures. The configuration of concentric bands in *Island No. 10* (page 71) had been used earlier in a rectangular field in *Tomlinson Court Park* (page 23); now—as a square—it could maintain the same proportions throughout the field of the canvas. A comparable process of simplification can be seen in the way in which the pattern of *Delaware Crossing* (page 72) squares off the design of *"Die Fahne hoch"* (page 19) while at the same time filling out the square implicit in *Ouray* (page 65). *Hampton Roads* (page 74) provides the entire pattern from which *Creede* (page 66) might have been cut, while the exclusively horizontal banding of *Palmito Ranch* (page 74)—the simplest configuration in the group—is a distillation of the banded transitional pictures, such as *Astoria* (page 14), which preceded the Black series.

Not all of the Benjamin Moore pictures refer back to designs in earlier work. The diagonals of *Sabine Pass* (page 75), while construable as fragments of the diamond-patterned Black pictures, more importantly point in a new direction that Stella was soon to explore. And the maze design of *New Madrid* (page 75), a configuration totally without precedent in Stella's earlier work, was soon to be used—with all its corners mitered—as a vehicle for his first multicolored paintings (see below pp. 76–78).

Stella had been working toward the tighter facture of the Benjamin Moore series all along. We have already observed how the drawing of the Aluminum pictures was more rigorous than that of the Black ones and the surfaces more even. The Copper pictures were, in turn, even more crisp in execution, since the copper metallic paint did not—as did the aluminum—spread slightly at the

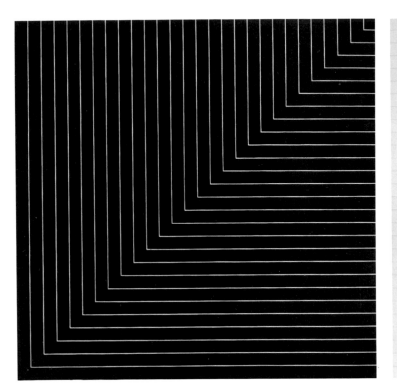

edges of the bands. But the copper paint also enjoyed a rich light inflection—particularly after some oxidation—that counteracted the tightness of its facture. The Benjamin Moore alkyd paint was absolutely matte and static in its surface, and the general tightness of the facture of the series was intensified by Stella's narrowing of the unpainted spaces between the bands. In the Aluminum and Copper series this had been approximately 1/8 of an inch; now it was reduced to about 1/16 of an inch.

It is not without significance that the square Benjamin Moore pictures should have followed hard upon the Copper series. From the most radically shaped of his fields, Stella had turned to the most simple. But if this might be considered a retreat from the point of view of the exploration of perimeter, it was an excellent context in which to begin the exploration of color. Not that these new pictures were multicolored. Like the earlier series, they were all monochrome. But the Black, Aluminum, and Copper pictures had belonged to the world of neutral anti-color, or pure light-dark, as befitted an art which, though it, in effect, turned drawing inside out (see above, p. 18), remained a linear one.

The square pictures were, in turn, red, orange, yellow, blue, green, and purple. Stella did not mix these colors himself, but used them as they came from the

left
Hampton Roads. (1961)
Alkyd on canvas, 6′5″ x 6′5″

right
Palmito Ranch. (1961)
Alkyd on canvas, 6′5″ x 6′5″

left
Sabine Pass. (1961)
Alkyd on canvas, 6'5'' x 6'5''

right
New Madrid. (1961)
Alkyd on canvas, 6'5'' x 6'5''

manufacturer. Later he would speak of trying "to keep the paint as good as it was in the can."[80] The choice of hues was obviously methodical—the three primaries and their secondaries—and a comparable spirit was reflected in the bland character of the commercial alkyd paint ("it had the nice dead kind of color that I wanted") which reinforced the stasis that is the hallmark of this series. Stella felt that the dominance of the design element rendered the choice of color arbitrary in the sense that it would not matter which of the six colors were applied to any particular pattern. And indeed, as if to demonstrate this fact, he executed a series of thirty-six 1-foot square versions of the designs— each one in all six colors.

IN THE LATTER PART of 1962 and the first months of the following year, Stella was occupied with a number of pictures which did not constitute a clearly defined series but were variations on two configurations of the Benjamin Moore group—the concentric squares of *Island No. 10* and the maze of *New Madrid.* In *Jasper's Dilemma* (page 77), based on the maze of *New Madrid,* diagonals were drawn from the corners of the canvas to the edges of the first "step" of the maze, thus dividing the concentric bands into four mitered segments.

The new pictures were executed in a number of different sizes up to the 85-inch square *Cato Manor* (page 81). The basic sequence, as in all configurations in this series, was a succession of five concentric bands around the central square, which could then be extended in multiples of this group. In the handling of these sequences Stella established two important new departures: in some cases he introduced sequences of differing light values and in others, sequences of differing hues.

The earlier pictures had been both monochrome and restricted to a single value (except, of course, for the unpainted interstitial strips, and for the uneven reflections of the black enamel and the metallic paint). In some of the new pictures Stella divided the six successive units of the basic sequence into six equidistant values from black to white on the gray scale. Pictures formed from two concentrically arranged basic sequences within a single square contained bands that moved from black to white and back to black again; the largest were formed from three basic units and simply carried the pattern back to white. Any of these groupings of the basic sequence could be reversed. The outer band of *Cato Manor*, for example, is black while the center square is white; just the reverse is true of *Sharpesville* (page 80).

The steplike succession of gray values in these pictures carried with it, for the first time in Stella's work, an implication of recessional space which relates to his speculations regarding sculpture (see above, pp. 68–70). The basic sequence suggested a kind of ziggurat or bellows, and the larger, multiple-sequence pictures implied a more complex in-and-out movement of the space. Not all these pictures were equally successful. By and large, those which anchored the framing edge with a black band worked best.

The same methodical spirit that led Stella to choose six values spanning the gray scale for the basic sequence of certain of the new pictures prompted his decision to use six colors (the three primaries and three secondaries) for other pictures in the series. These, in turn, were precisely the six colors that he had used in the different paintings of the Benjamin Moore series. The order of the colors was spectral, beginning with red and passing through orange, yellow, green, and blue to purple. (William Seitz's color wheel had hung in Stella's studio since his Princeton days; Barbara Rose remembers it as "a kind of talisman.") These six alkyd hues—so different in character from artists' colors—gave the pictures the naïve aspect of a child's crayon drawing, and Stella himself has spoken of the color application as recalling the spirit of a child's primer. "The reason I used color that way at first," he says, "was to fit the new work into the whole thinking of the striped pictures in general. I wanted to use a fairly formalized, programmatic kind of color."

Jasper's Dilemma. (1962–63)
Alkyd on canvas, 6'5" x 12'10"

76

The power of the governing pattern was such that it held the pictures together. But the design survived the color more than it was supported by it. It is not surprising that the color pictures were less successful than those in black, white, and gray, for the color system did not lock into the governing pattern as the value progression did. It seemed attached to the pictures in a somewhat inorganic way.

In the first instance, this problem followed from the fact that color is not quantitative whereas surface design is. In addition, the interrelationships of different colors are not as readily perceivable as those between lights and darks of the same color. It is, therefore, impossible to program or structure color successfully in the same a priori sequential manner as light and dark. The relationships expressed by the color "triangle" of the primaries and secondaries, or the color "circle" of the spectral hues, are abstractions of a more theoretical order than are the units on the gray scale, and making color "work" is more a question of pure intuition. While the mind may know, for example, that two colors are complementary, their co-operation is not as readily recognizable as are relationships of value.

Moreover, since the values of the six hues chosen by Stella did not line up in a consistent light-dark sequence, the effect was to dissociate the spatial implications of the design structure from those of the color scheme. These problems were even further compounded in the pictures based on the maze pattern. This design was complicated enough in its light-dark form; with color added, it became almost impossible to decipher, however coherent it may have been from a purely intellectual point of view.

Considering the colored maze paintings according to the dialectic of problem-solving which Stella himself uses, we would have to say that he had failed to solve the problem of uniting a variety of color juxtapositions with this most complicated of his design structures. The same pattern in black, grays, and white functioned to much better advantage. Stella had mistakenly tried to handle color in the same methodical manner in which he had ordered his light-dark structure. These two articulations of the same design were presented most dramatically in visual terms in *Jasper's Dilemma* (page 77), where the format is a rectangle that contains two adjacent mazes, one in values, the other in hues. The title refers to the fact that Jasper Johns had often alternated between grisaille and color in realizing a particular design. If the interchangeability of grisaille and color presented problems for Johns, one suspects that Stella was facing similar ones, and that *Jasper's Dilemma* was, as it were, an exposition of them.

That Stella was to some extent critically aware of this problem is suggested by the fact that after this series, he gave up the use of polychromy. During the

Les Indes galantes (B & W sketch). (1962) Alkyd on canvas, 5'11½" x 5'11½"

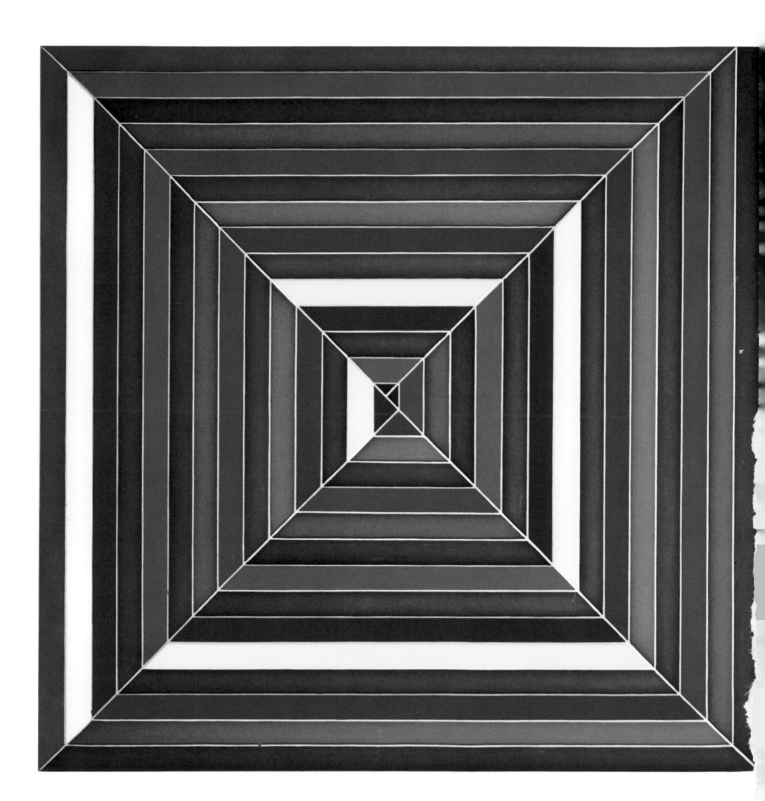

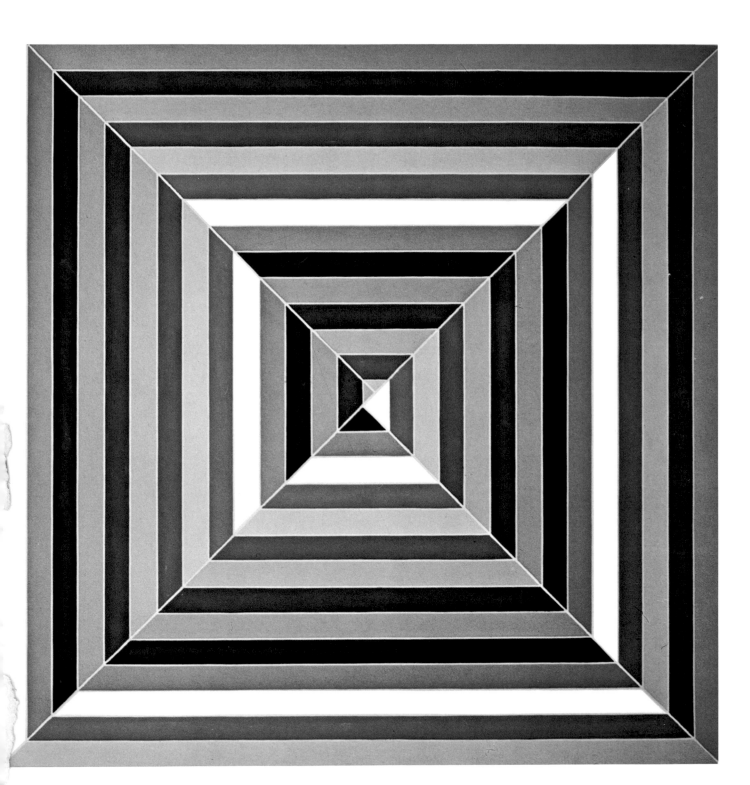

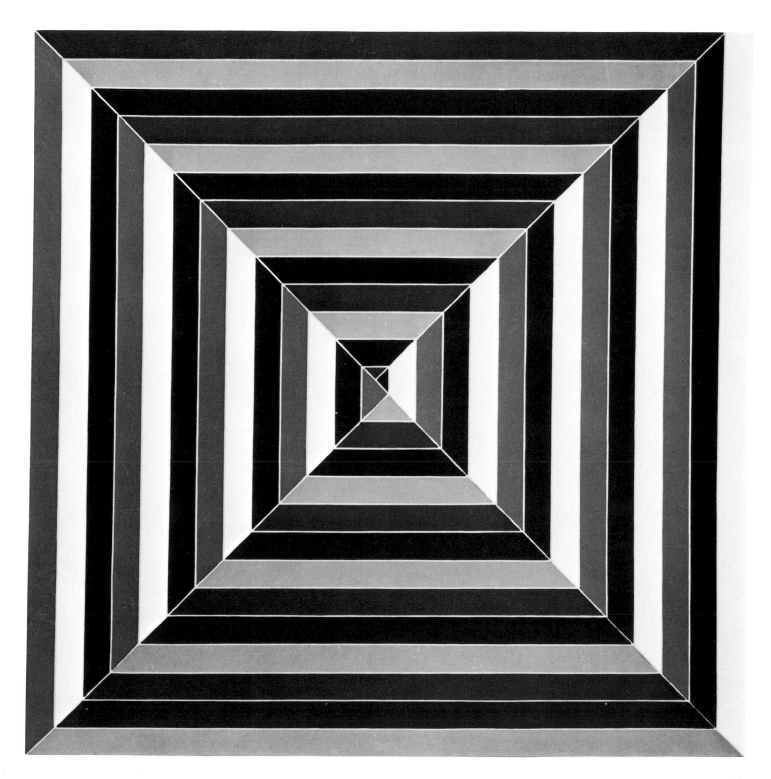

79

Sharpesville. (1962). Alkyd on canvas, 7′1′′ x 7′1′′

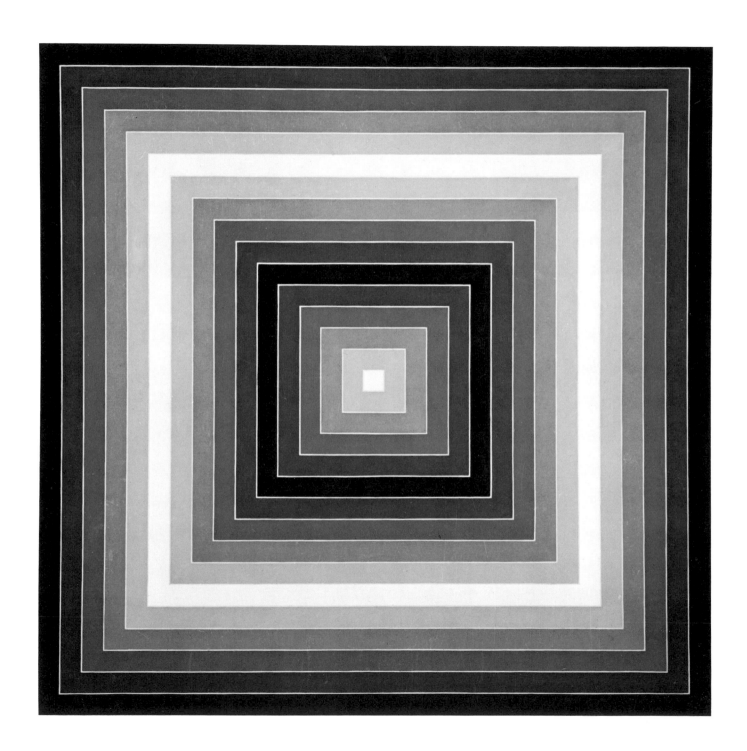

Cato Manor. (1962). Alkyd on canvas, 7'1'' x 7'1''

next three years he worked his way back into color—this time very success-fully—in quite a different manner. In speaking of his polygonal color pictures of 1966, Stella indicated that he had learned a lesson from the work of 1962. "I can think about color as much as I want," he stated to Aian Solomon, "but thinking about color abstractly hasn't done me any real good. I'm not able to solve or to analyze color in a way that you might say that I've been able to do more successfully with structure. . . . I mean I don't know what color analysis would be as far as painting is concerned anyway. . . . Structural analysis is a matter of describing the way the picture is organized. Color analysis would seem to be saying what you think the color does. And it seems to me that you are more likely to get an area of common agreement in the former."[81]

In the Benjamin Moore pictures and their offshoots (the grisaille and multi-colored concentric squares and mitered mazes), Stella had retreated from the problems of perimeter in order to explore other possibilities. In the latter half of 1963, however, he returned to the shaped canvas with a vengeance in a series of metallic purple[82] polygonal pictures—among them a trapezoid, a penta-gon, a hexagon, and a triangle. In these, the contour of the perimeter was echoed not only by the interior bands, which paralleled it on all sides, but by the removal of the same shape from the center of the field, turning the painting, in effect, into a kind of "frame" for a polygonal area of wall that showed through. This polygonal wall area, by recapitulating the framing edge of the picture, gave the greatest emphasis yet seen in Stella's work to the shape of the framing edge. In *Avicenna* (page 49) Stella had surrounded a "hole" in the field on all sides. But the central notch of *Avicenna* was so small that the shadow cast by the deep stretcher did not allow the wall to show through adequately; thus, the attempt to equate its space with those of the notches at its four corners was abortive. In the new polygonal pictures, the space removed from the interior of the field was equal to one half of the painted area surrounding it, and the problem of the cast shadow was minimized.

The Purple pictures were all named after friends. The assignments of the particular shapes—Carl Andre is a rhombus, Sidney Guberman (page 88) is a hexagon—remain the painter's private jokes. But Stella even extended these meanings to the relationship between two people; thus the triangle of *Leo Cas-telli* (page 86) was seen by him alternatively as part of a larger triangle of which *Ileana Sonnabend* (page 87) formed the remaining trapezoid.

In returning to the shaped canvas, Stella also returned to monochromy. All the polygonal "portraits" were of a rather noxious metallic purple ("I was looking for a very vulgar color," Stella recalls); but the color was not fast, and over the years these pictures have faded to a very light lavender. In his concise and

Henry Garden. (1963)
Metallic paint on canvas,
6'8" x 6'8"

Charlotte Tokayer. (1963)
Metallic paint on canvas,
7'3" x 7'7½"

View of exhibition at Leo Castelli Gallery, New York, January–February 1964

superbly written monograph on Stella, Robert Rosenblum speaks of these pictures in their original hue in terms of a "new color fluorescence which smacked of the growing sensibility in the 1960s to the commercial, acid hues that found their way into much Pop art of the period" and to "the metallic, spray-gunned paint surfaces of John Chamberlain's automobile-fragment sculptures. . . ."[83] But while Pop Art itself absorbed ideas from Stella—Wesselmann's shaped canvases, for example—it would be a mistake to stress affinities between the two enterprises. "I kind of like Pop Art in a relaxed way," Stella observes,

and we share certain things (many of us are about the same age). But I don't have the Pop artists' literary attitude about things and their use. I mean, I wouldn't use fluorescent color literally because it's like a billboard, or something like that. I don't find billboards interesting except as billboards. . . . Pop Art doesn't make me think particularly about painting—and nothing to do with it influences the way I make pictures.

Whatever the motivation behind the choice of the metallic purple, that color played a much greater expressive role than did the aluminum and copper anti-colors of the earlier shaped canvases. Thus, though the shaped formats of the purple pictures mark the end of a progression implicit in the Black series and explicit in the Aluminum series, these paintings represent a new beginning in their emphasis on the affective role of color. Despite the explorations in sequential polychromy which followed the Benjamin Moore series, "the real shift

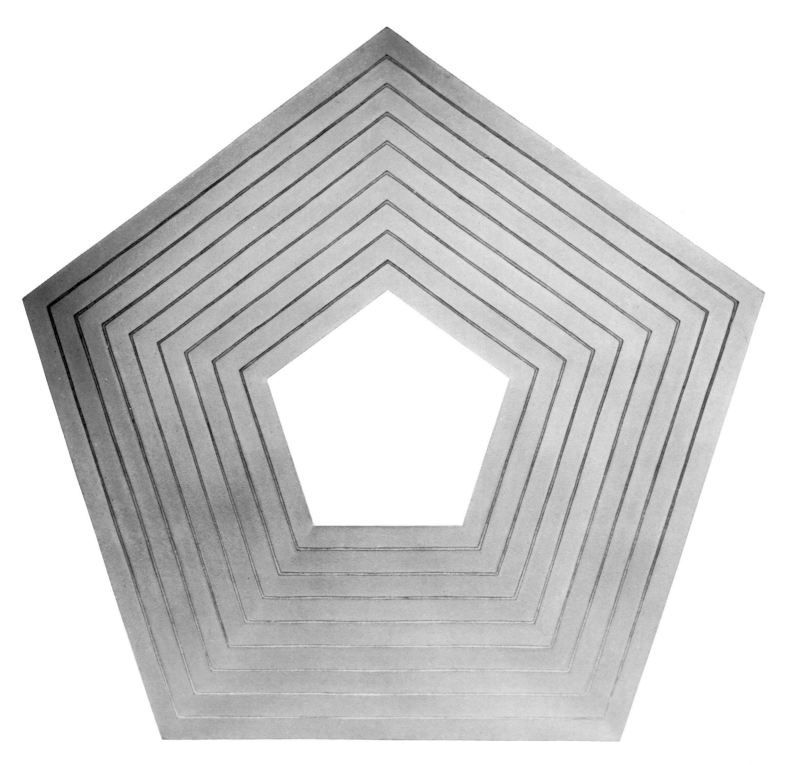

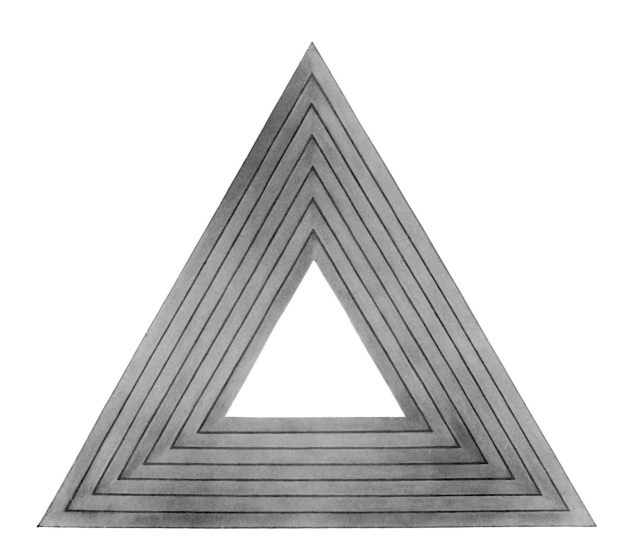

Leo Castelli. (1963). Metallic paint on canvas, 7′5″ x 8′3″

Ileana Sonnabend. (1963). Metallic paint on canvas, 6′5¾″ x 10′8″

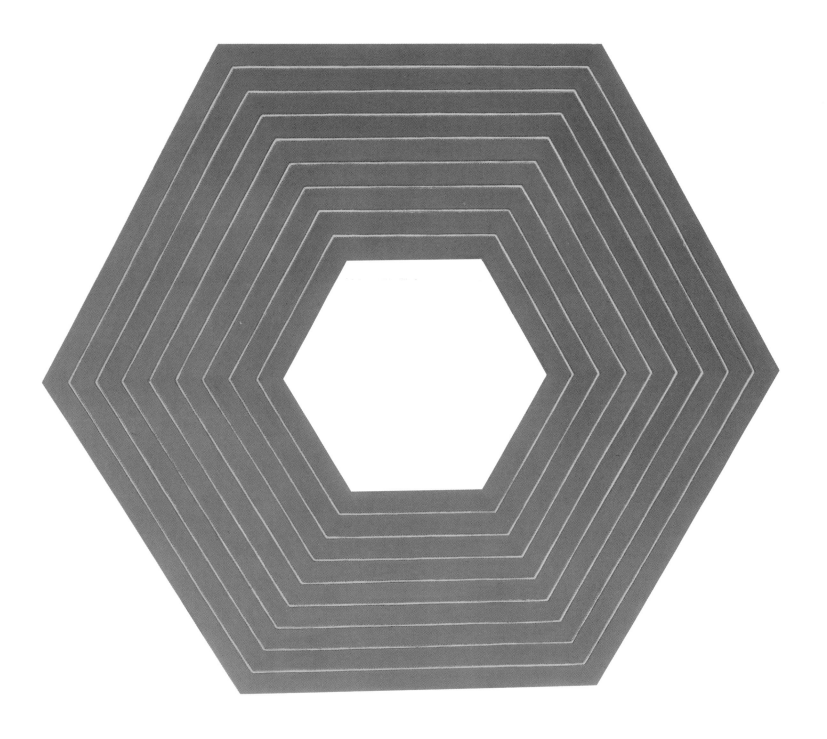

88

to color came with the purple pictures," Stella observes. "I think that is where I became really committed to color in a funny kind of way—one in which I couldn't avoid it."

THE COMMONLY HELD view of Stella's career divides it into two phases: the first begins with the 1958 stripe paintings; the second, with the color polygons of 1966. I believe, however, that this view somewhat oversimplifies the lines of his development. It attributes to the irregularly shaped color polygons of 1966 (see pages 110–128) a more complete break with their predecessors than they actually represent. In so doing, it overlooks a less obvious but crucial change that came about at the end of 1963 following the polygonal "portraits." The intervening pictures of 1964–65, while still banded, handle the striping and shaping in a very new way; they also demonstrate a taste for large, sensuous areas of color that would be the point of departure for the pictures of the following years.

Stella's development from the Black through the Purple series impresses one in retrospect by the taut step-by-step logic with which it unfolds (despite the tangential offshoots from the Benjamin Moore pictures). But from 1964 onward there is a relaxation in his approach to pictorial problems, a tendency to explore different and even contradictory approaches simultaneously and to reach back into his own past to take up possibilities that had not been fully realized. We may compare this with the way in which the extraordinarily focused and closed progress of Picasso's Analytic Cubism from 1908–12 gave way to his more open, eclectic approach during the years following. By 1964 Stella felt less pressure to "march forward," more freedom to work back and forth over his own ideas. ("If I don't have access to them, what do I have access to?")

This *détente* was certainly a result of the painter's own judgment that his particular conception of picture-making had been convincingly established, and that it was now embodied in a sufficient number of successful pictures to allow him to step back and get some distance from himself. His painting through 1963 had been primarily engaged with structure and with the need to prove his structures viable. Now he would turn more to color. Cerebration would gradually recede in favor of intuition and sensation. "Up through the purple paintings," Stella asserts,

my pictures were definitely involved in a specific attitude toward painting—and certain attendant formal and technical problems. They were also involved with the problem of establishing a painterly identity—what it is to be a painter and make paintings—and with the subjective, emotional responses to that situation. I don't think any painter can get around this. It has finally to do with the way

Valparaiso Flesh and Green.
(1963). Metallic paint on canvas,
6'6'' x 11'3¼''

View of exhibition at Galerie Lawrence, Paris, April 1963

*you see yourself, what you do, and the world around you. It seems to me that
these works had a fairly consistent kind of attitude, and there's no question that
they were somehow directly involved with things outside me—they had a little
bit more of an ax to grind in just about every way. Something about color painting
is more open, and slightly more—just about painting.*

While artist-in-residence at Dartmouth College in the summer of 1963, Stella
began "to open up with color and metallic surface at the same time." Metallic
color, as we have seen, has a unique character which is at variance with both
non-metallic color and metallic anti-colors, such as aluminum. Metallic apple
green, for example, which Stella used in *Valparaiso Green* (page 93), can be
matched in tone by making a kind of gray-green with artists' colors. But without
the metallic particles, it is simply not the same color.

Apart from the extra-pictorial associations metallic paints elicit—and pictorially
they fly in the face of a *belle peinture* tradition, owing to their relative vulgarity—
they perform technically in a way that helped Stella as he began to re-explore
color. Metallic paint operates in a special manner. The paint itself sits in the
weave of the canvas, but the metallic particles radiate a sheen of light that seems
almost independent of the body of the color, as if situated ever so slightly in

90

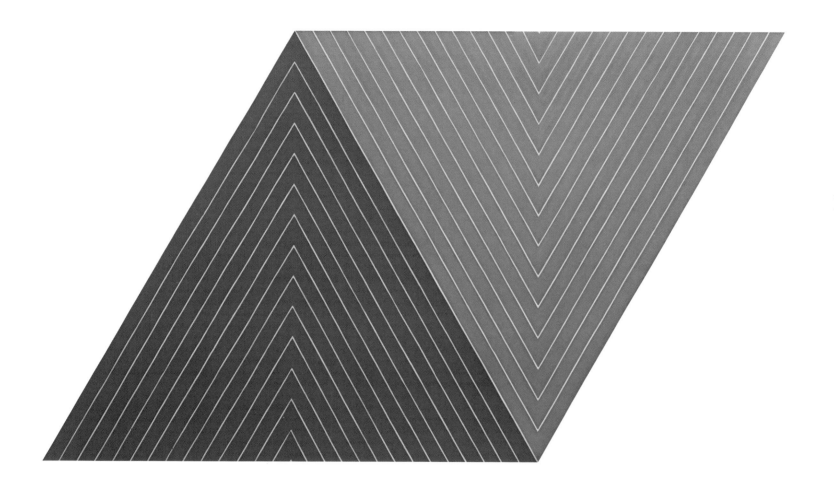

front of the canvas itself. The effect of this sheen is simultaneoulsy somewhat to "gray out" an individual color and to produce a kind of uniform luminosity—a tonal unity—when different metallic colors are juxtaposed. In the concentric squares and mitered mazes, where Stella used the non-metallic spectral colors in a methodical way, it was precisely this unity that had eluded him. Now he was starting all over again with color, and in *Valparaiso Flesh and Green* (page 91) the juxtaposition of large areas of approximate complementaries was made smoother by the unifying effect of the all-over sheen. But it was precisely these technical properties of metallic paint that became more and more limiting as Stella's mastery of color grew. By the time he needed a fuller range of hue, value, and chroma, he had shifted to epoxy and fluorescent paint.

The shapes of the Valparaiso pictures—large trapezoids and parallelograms—were more like rectangular fields than like the shaped canvases of the Copper and Purple series, essentially because they had much more interior space. The large, alternating triangular areas were virtual color fields, although they were still characteristically subdivided into stripes. Stella continued to find this modular articulation necessary because metallic paint, in large areas, created an "absolute kind of brushiness" that he wanted to avoid. "I could never control that," Stella observes, "and wasn't much interested in the effect." It was not surprising, therefore, that when he moved into his personal counterpart of color-field painting two years later, he abandoned metallic paint.

DURING HIS SUMMER at Dartmouth, Stella also painted some pictures that were more radically shaped than the Valparaiso group. These were arrived at by joining wedge- or chevron-shaped areas of stripes. In *Polk City* (page 94), for example, two such areas are placed back to back; in *Plant City* (page 95) four of them join at the center of what becomes a star-shaped painting. These pictures, which were executed in metal primers—zinc chromate and red lead—rather than metallic paints, were all of single colors, but they opened the way for a brilliant series (begun in the fall of 1964) in which the triangles of the Valparaiso paintings, their bottom centers cut out to form vector-like V's, would be juxtaposed successfully in as many as four different colors.

The simplest of these "Notched V" compositions were those composed of a single V, such as the royal blue *Slieve More* (1964).[84] In *Itata* (page 99) the blue V is joined to another V in a coppery red (known commercially as Brilliant Fire), forming a kind of Z-shaped silhouette—the counterpart in this series to the earlier *Polk City*. In *Itata,* the tips of the vector areas—and hence their bands—face in opposite directions, while in the arrow-like black and green *Ifafa II* (page 98), the traveling of the bands has a single focus. *Quathlamba* (page

Valparaiso Green. (1963) Metallic paint on canvas, 6'5" x 14'10"

92

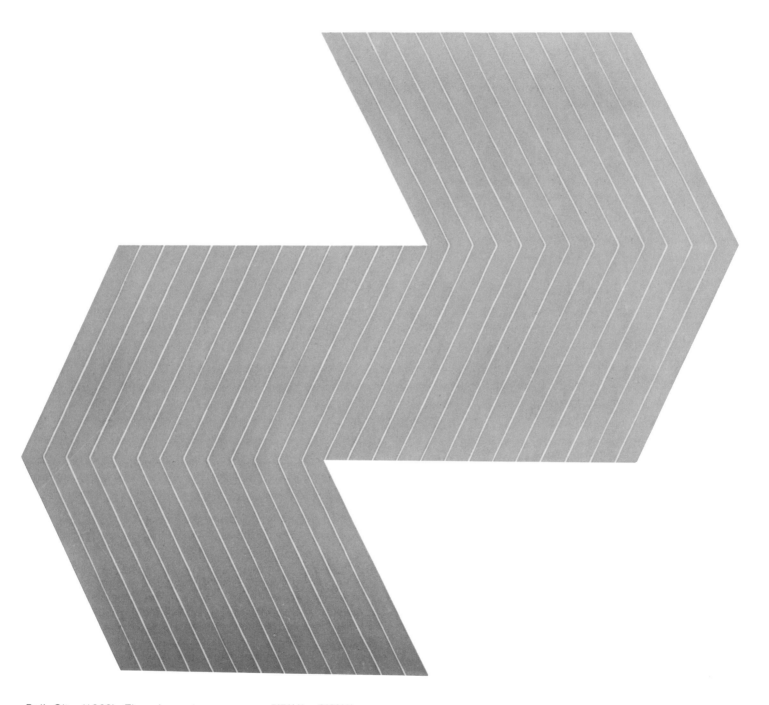

Polk City. (1963). Zinc chromate on canvas, 5′7½′′ x 8′8¼′′

opposite
Plant City. (1963). Zinc chromate on canvas, 8′ x 8′

94

95

Tampa. (1963)
Red lead on canvas,
8'3⅜" x 8'3⅜"

102) locks these opposing thrusts together, the green V in the center moving convergently with the red V on the right and divergently from the blue one on the left.

In *Quathlamba* and the four-color *Empress of India* (page 100) Stella's ability to handle the polychrome picture was demonstrated as never before. To be sure, the value range in all of them was extremely narrow, and—with the exception of the prophetic *Empress of India*—all the colors stayed close to the primaries, but this was in part necessitated by the radical shaping. In the face of these complicated silhouettes, the inherent limitations of the metallic paints—their restricted range of values and intensities—became a virtue. "The value scale of metallic color," Stella observes,

from its lightest to where it becomes dark or black is relatively limited. You begin to notice this once you use more than two or three colors because they all tend to be alike. . . . But in these pictures I felt this was working for me because they were so radically shaped. . . . Any jumping around in the color—any big change in value or intensity—and I would have been in a lot of trouble. When you have four vectored V's moving against each other, if one jumps out, you dislocate the plane and destroy the whole thing entirely.

As we noticed earlier, the successions of jogs in the bands of Stella's Aluminum series acted as vectors creating a continuous ripple that moved the eye diagonally across the surface of the picture, the whole of which was conceived as a "force field." These ripple movements involved only those relatively small areas where breaks in the direction of the band or stripe pattern took place; the rest of the field was static. In the Notched V pictures this limited ripple has given way to the suggestion of entire surfaces in motion. Each V is not simply a vector in a field; it comprises a field itself. And the equilibrium of the painting is achieved by a precise counterbalancing of these dynamic areas and forces. Stella has spoken of them as "flying wedge" pictures—no reference to football intended—a term that conjures an image of the V-shaped flying wing designs for the supersonic transports. Robert Rosenblum has referred to the "velocity of [Stella's] diagonal stripes" as "clean and breathless as a jet take-off."[85] He considers that

the wedge-shaped canvas, with its swift ascent of convergent (or descent of divergent) stripes, is almost a twentieth-century symbol for abstract, mechanized speed, whose lineage could be traced through the streamlining in commercial machine design of the 1920s and 1930s (in everything from hubcaps to refrigerators) back to the "lines of force" in Italian Futurist art. And even the icy

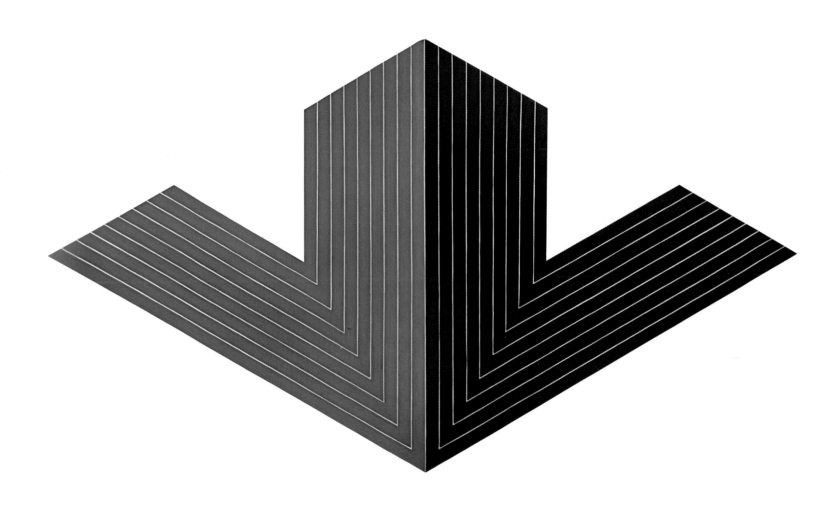

Ifafa II. (1964). Metallic powder in polymer emulsion on canvas, 6'4¾'' x 11'2¾''

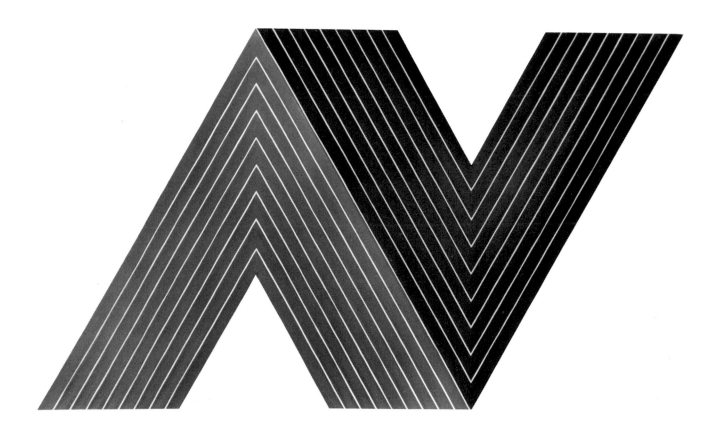

Itata. (1964). Metallic powder in polymer emulsion on canvas, 6'4½'' x 11'4¼''

colors . . . conform to this mechanized imagery that provides, as it were, an abstract counterpart to the more explicit use of industrial reproductive techniques (Ben-Day dots, commercial paints, stencils) in much Pop art of the mid-1960s.[86]

Rosenblum also speaks of "the basic unit" of Stella's "vector of concentric chevrons" as "analogous to the V-shaped thrusts of color in Kenneth Noland's chevron paintings of 1963–4."[87] This analogy is meant, of course, in only the most general terms, for the derivations and nature of the two seemingly related geometries are very different. In Noland's work, the entire picture contains one chevron, and the structure of the picture depends upon the relationships between the differing colors of each of its bands. In Stella's paintings, each entire chevron has only one color (close to the primaries and very different from the color of Noland), and the structure of the picture is determined by the juxtaposition of multiple chevrons. Noland's chevrons marked his opening into a symmetrical V-shape of the bands of his earlier concentric circles; he has since bent the two sides of his chevron down to form horizontal bands. Stella's V-shaped forms derive from an interest in the triangle that goes back to Black paintings like *Point of Pines* of 1959 (page 35) and which was taken up again in the polygonal "portraits."

IN THEIR COMBINATION of polychromy and marked shaping, the Notched V paintings stand at the center of Stella's concerns during 1964–65. He worked on two other series during these years. The first was a group of pictures (named after Moroccan cities) that were executed entirely in fluorescent paint on square formats—pictures in which considerations of color were paramount. The other was a set of large monochromatic striped pictures titled after colloquial Spanish expressions and executed in metallic paints. These "Running V" paintings, as Stella calls them, summarized the explorations of tracking and shaping that began in the Aluminum series of 1960.

Adelante of 1964 (page 103) is characteristic of the latter group, most of which were shown at the Kasmin Gallery in London late in that year. Just as the polychromy of the Notched V pictures reinforced their articulation of the thrust and counterthrust of multiple fields, so the monochromy of the blue-gray *Adelante* reflected the fact that the tracking followed a path across a single field— inflected but unbroken. Horizontal on the left, it dips and rises chevron-like in the center, and establishes symmetry by returning to the horizontal on the right. In the Aluminum series the shifts in tracking—the jogs—were all at right angles, and the sense of movement was limited to the vector pattern created by their serial repetition. In *Adelante* the entire field has become a single giant vector.

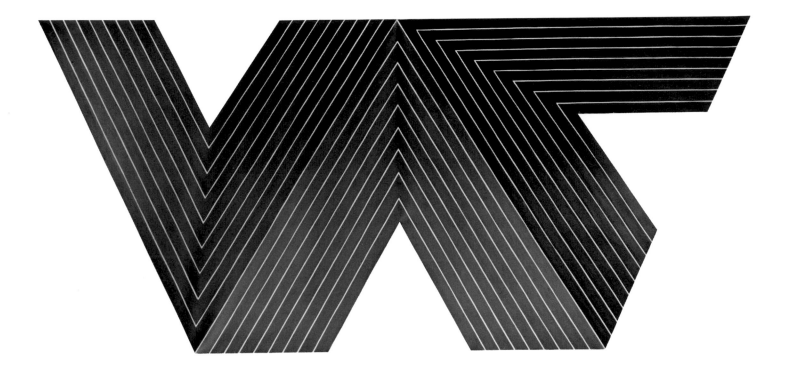

The paintings in the Kasmin exhibition were notable for the width of what Rosenblum has called "pictorial highways (as many as twenty-seven lanes wide!)."[88] But the climax of the group was a more narrow picture of extraordinary length, the nearly 24-foot long *De la nada Vida a la nada Muerte* (page 105) executed in 1965 in metallic brass paint. The predominant movement of the twenty parallel stripes of this picture is horizontal. But that movement is twice interrupted by a variation on the V-shape which detours the tracking of the bands upward on the left and downward on the right. *De la nada Vida* epitomizes the extent to which Stella had abandoned the synoptic, single-image reading that his earlier pictures had demanded. And while we must experience this long picture as a single entity to understand it fully, there is no question that the visualization of its entirety is constantly challenged by the tendency to read the picture—virtually in narrative fashion—from left to right along the tracking of the bands. Two years later, in the 42-foot long *Sangre de Cristo,* Stella created a picture that virtually defies a synoptic reading.[89]

In the Aluminum pictures, the change in angle at which the metallic paint reflects the light at each jog reinforces a slight illusion of ripple on the surface. While similar changes in reflection suggest some folding of the surface in all

Quathlamba. (1964)
Metallic powder in polymer emulsion on canvas,
6'5" x 13'7"

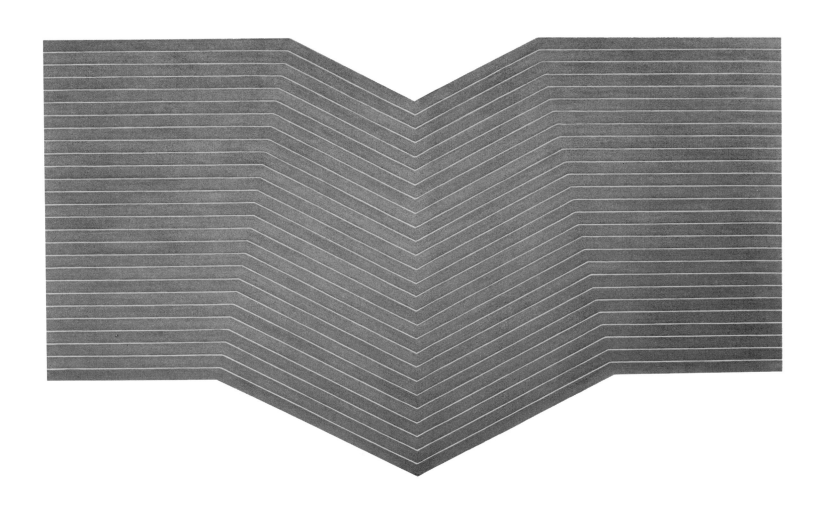

Adelante. (1964). Metallic powder in polymer emulsion on canvas, 8'¼'' x 13'9½''

the pictures of the Running V series, the impression of an illusion of spatial recession or projection is strongest in *De la nada Vida.* Here, the four areas of diagonal tracking that lead the horizontal bands into the two V-shapes tend somewhat to be read as moving either forward or backward from the picture plane.

However, the illusion created in *De la nada Vida* by the combination of value change in the metallic paint and the shifting contours of the picture's silhouette is countered by the fact that the bands of the composition are parallel rather than convergent—as they would be in paintings with illusionist perspective, whether representational or abstract. This parallelism functions to absorb optical suggestions of convexity and concavity into the prevailing two-dimensionality of the configuration as a whole. Had that assimilation not been achieved to Stella's satisfaction, he could have side-stepped the issue by brushing the diagonal bands so that their metallic particles lay in the same direction as those of the horizontal bands, thus precluding shifts in their light values.

At the opposite end of the spectrum from the Running V series were the contemporaneous Moroccan pictures. Here, a new emphasis on color was achieved by eliminating the shaping of the canvas—a component that would have contended with the color for the viewer's attention—and by the exclusive use of fluorescent Day-Glo paints. These are more luminous than the enamel, chromate, or metallic paints that Stella had previously employed and are available in a greater range of hues. The alternating red and yellow bands of *Marrakech* (page 106) and the green and yellow ones of *Fez* (page 109) produce an effect of brightness and transparency new in Stella's art. The transparency resulted from the fact that in the pictures of this series he applied the paint, for the first time, in a single layer that formed an almost bodiless film. Though still banded, the Moroccan pictures read fundamentally differently from the earlier monochromatic striped compositions in that the configurations are perceived in terms of the color bands themselves, independently of the narrow unpainted areas between them. The latter now function purely as breathing spaces.

In *Marrakech,* the root of the configuration is the Greek cross pattern of *Delaware Crossing* (page 72). In the latter, the quadrants are made up of sequential bands that each make one right-angle turn. But in *Marrakech* an X formed of the two diagonals of the square field is superimposed on the cross. These diagonals cut each of the bands in mitered fashion at the center of their turns, and the two segments of each band are painted alternately yellow and red. The resulting pattern creates a slight illusion of folding along the line of the diagonal axes, a skirting around the edges of illusionism which is the coun-

De la nada Vida a la nada Muerte. (1965). Metallic powder in polymer emulsion on canvas, 7' x 23'5¾''

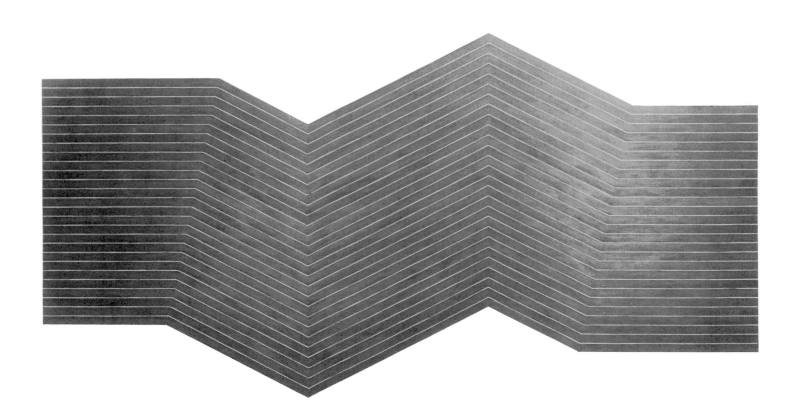

Nunca pasa nada. (1964)
Metallic powder in polymer
emulsion on canvas,
ca. 9′ x 18′

terpart, in the Moroccan series, of the ambiguous spatial suggestions of *De la nada Vida.*

The Moroccan series began with two-color pictures like *Marrakech* but reached its climax in *Sidi Ifni* of 1965 (page 108)—by far the most ambitious of his color undertakings up to that time. In this painting Stella succeeded in making ten different Day-Glo hues function together. The configuration returns to an idea present in the Black pictures of 1959. Like *Jill* (page 33), it consists of a diamond pattern inscribed on a square format, the corners filled out with bands parallel to those of the central motif. Then, in *Sidi Ifni,* the field (and hence the diamond bands) is divided into eight segments by a combination of diagonal, vertical, and horizontal bisectors. The bands in each of the eight subdivisions alternate a yellow with a darker color (reading clockwise, crimson, charcoal, orange, purple, brown, green, pink, and blue). The principle of alternation also applies to the yellow. Two yellows are used—a lemon and a Naples yellow—and they are alternately paired with one of the darker hues in successive subdivisions of the composition.

THE ADMISSION OF various forms of marginal or potential illusionism into the Running V's and the Moroccan pictures of 1964–65 had been anticipated in 1962, in paintings such as *Cato Manor* (page 81). However, the irregular geometries and mitered bands of the 1966 Polygons posed even more centrally the problem of ambiguities in the spatial readings. Taken together all these works reflect considerable tempering of the posture taken in Stella's Black pictures. The symmetrical—or "non-relational"—and synoptic structure of the early series had gone hand in hand with maximal flattening of the space; such vestiges of space as remained were controlled through the regularity of the serial pattern. These aims had been realized to Stella's most complete satisfaction in the Benjamin Moore paintings, but to that extent, the series represented a dead end, and everything Stella did afterward was engaged in an opening outward. Subsequent advances in drawing and coloring were made through the admission, if only tacit, that painting is necessarily to some degree an art of illusion, and that its inevitable ambiguities can be put to pictorial advantage. Not that Stella would ever become an Abstract Illusionist. He has never resorted to modeling or perspective devices—linear or atmospheric. But in certain aspects of the Irregular Polygons of 1966 in particular, Stella seems to have shown an awareness of the possibilities—as well as the problems—of spatial suggestion and has made them work for him.

THE IRREGULAR POLYGONS marked an important turn in Stella's development. The salient characteristic of the series is the interpenetration of contrasting geo-

107

108

Fez. (1964). Fluorescent alkyd on canvas, 6′5″ x 6′5″

opposite
Sidi Ifni. (1965). Fluorescent alkyd on canvas, 7′ 4″ x 7′3¾″

110

Effingham I. (Second version, 1967). Fluorescent alkyd and epoxy paint on canvas, 10'8" x 11'

metrical shapes, the latter treated as fields of color (unbroken by stripes) whose hues are chosen on the basis of intuition rather than method. These pictures differ fundamentally, however, from "color-field" painting as that term has been used to describe the work of artists such as Louis, Noland, and Olitski, or applied retroactively to that of Rothko and Newman. Color is the primary element in the painting of all these artists, and the configuration is arrived at as the color itself suggests to the artist the quantity, weight, expanse, and position proper to it. There are, of course, in the case of each of these artists, certain a priori formal conceptions within which these color relationships emerge. But whatever the general character of the image, the particular arrangement of a given picture follows from the desire to let the color express the emotional experience in the least inhibited way. In Stella's Irregular Polygons, however, the structure exists a priori and color is chosen to fit its fields.

Nevertheless, the success or failure of any picture in this series depends precisely on the rightness of the color combination. Since Stella was reluctant to overpaint, the improvising of color arrangements after work on a given picture had begun was precluded. He therefore decided to give himself that possibility in another manner. Stretchers were made in quadruplicate for each of the eleven shapes in the series, giving him four chances to explore different color combinations within each configuration. Sometimes a number of successful solutions for the same problem were found, one picture "breeding" another. In other cases, a successful picture was achieved through the understanding of a previous failure. Though the layouts of each of the four were exactly the same, the different color choices from picture to picture created a wide range in their expressive character. The decision to make four paintings in each image was arbitrary. "It's just the number I thought I'd like to have . . . to work on one shape," Stella noted at the time.

If I don't like the way one comes out, I can go on to the next one. And it also gives me something to work against. . . . It doesn't matter whether the first painting of each shape is good or bad—it gives me a start. If I see in it something that I like—or something that I don't like—it's still something to react against and it sets the way I'll go with the next few pictures.[90]

The eleven shapes of the series were selected from a larger number of sketches that Stella had been accumulating for some years. And while all eleven could be interpreted as exploring the theme of the *interpenetration* of *contrasting* geometrical shapes—as opposed to that of the *juxtaposition* of *similar* shapes that had prevailed in the Notched V's—the very marked differences in structure tend to divide the configurations into three groups. In order to discuss these

Chocorua I. (1966)
Fluorescent alkyd and epoxy
paint on canvas, 10' x 10'8''

View of exhibition at Leo Castelli Gallery, New York, March–April 1966

differences, I should like to adopt the terminology established by Michael Fried in his searching analysis of these pictures. Fried noted at the outset that the major difference between this series and all Stella's earlier shaped canvases was that the absolute identity of surface pattern and canvas shape (or picture support) no longer existed. To facilitate discussion, he therefore distinguished between the "silhouette of the support," which he characterized as "literal shape," and "the outlines of elements in a given picture," which he called "depicted shape."[91]

Measured by the complexity of relationships between literal and depicted shapes, the Irregular Polygons range from the simplicity of the Chocorua configuration to the complexity of the Sanbornville and Sunapee formats. This is not, however, to imply that the simplest were conceived or executed first; surprisingly for Stella, the order of realization bore no relation to the complexity of the configuration.

Chocorua I (page 113) states the central theme of the series in its most uncomplicated form. The dominant geometry is a compact gray rectangle that is very close to a square; a tan isosceles triangle has been inserted into its upper left corner. (This combination comes very close to being the most primary geometrical conjunction possible in the series—namely, the interpenetration of an equilateral triangle and a square.) The tan triangle, which is the smaller—one

might say weaker—geometrical unit in *Chocorua I,* is strengthened by an 8-inch peripetal band of white, the standard width for the bands in every configuration of the series. Wherever this triangular white band penetrates the field of the rectangle, it is met by a contiguous pink band that acts on behalf of the rectangle to cushion visually the impact of the triangle's insertion. The pink band runs not only along the inserted edge of the triangle but continues along the top and left side of the rectangle, thus giving extra support to those borders which receive the impact of the intrusion. But even as this pink band acts to cushion the triangle, it also functions as a visual spring, suggesting that a reciprocal pressure is being exerted by the rectangle against the triangle.

The power of the rectangle—its sense of wholeness and autonomy—is further enhanced by the mitering of the right and left terminals of the pink band. This fixes the corners of the rectangle more strongly and reinforces the impression that its unframed lower and right boundaries define a closed, discrete field, rather than a segment of what might be visualized as an extendable one. The bands of *Chocorua I* help insure the tension of its conflicting geometries by guaranteeing that we will not read the triangle as simply overlapping a section of the rectangle, in the manner of collage, but rather as pressing against it on the same plane in space. The dynamic is one of interpenetration, not overlapping.

Among the other configurations that fall into this simplest group of the Irregular Polygons—those based upon an interpenetration of two regular geometries—are Ossipee (a pentagon inserted into a parallelogram), Conway (a parallelogram inserted into a rectangle, and Moultonboro (a triangle inserted into a square).

Conway I (page 116) is slightly more elaborate in conception than *Chocorua I.* In the latter, the viewer is given some portion of all four sides of the rectangle and all three sides of the triangle in a *literal* manner—i.e., in terms of the framing shape of the field itself. The same is true for all four sides of the dominant rectangle of *Conway I.* But of the smaller parallelogram that interpenetrates that rectangle, we see parts of only three sides in literal terms. The missing side is implied by those literally given, but exists *only* in depicted form. Seeing the silhouette of the picture alone, one would tend to complete the three-sided form at the bottom as a parallelogram. But the *exact* size of parallelogram is not literally determined, as are the triangle and the rectangle of *Chocorua I.* In fact, the eye might well assume completion of the parallelogram at a point less high than it is actually depicted in *Conway I.*

The bands of *Conway I* perform in a more intricate manner than those of *Chocorua I.* The blue-green band around the blue parallelogram functions, as did the white band around *Chocorua*'s tan triangle, to strengthen the smaller geometrical form which is inserted into the dominant one. By the same token,

Tuftonboro II. (1966)
Fluorescent alkyd and epoxy
paint on canvas, 8'3" x 9'1"

Conway I. (1966)
Fluorescent alkyd and epoxy
paint on canvas, 6'8" x 10'2"

the gray band of *Conway I* that cushions the parallelogram's insertion functions like the pink band of *Chocorua I* in continuing onward to define two of the rectangle's sides. At this point, however, an important distinction emerges: where the gray band touches the upper right corner of the rectangle of *Conway I*, Stella did not miter its edge. In *Chocorua I*, this mitering had defined the upper right and lower left corners of the rectangle, thus further endowing its two unbanded sides with the quality of boundaries. Since none of the bands that terminate on the upper side of the rectangle of *Conway I* are mitered, that field of red color suggests a possibility of being continued upward, an extendability that contrasts with the appearance of finiteness in the gray rectangle of *Chocorua I*.

The coloring of *Conway I*—red, gray, pink, blue-green, and blue—is superb and marked a new level of accomplishment for Stella. While the color choices in the Irregular Polygons were, in general, intuitive, certain combinations such as the yellow, blue, and orange of *Effingham I* (page 110),[92] remained very close in spirit to the groupings of primaries and secondaries used in Stella's earlier work. The more unusual tonalities of *Conway I*, especially the harmonious combination of a normally jarring red and pink, involved a greater degree of invention and risk.

The red and pink of *Conway I* are Day-Glo colors, though their multi-layering makes them more opaque and different in tonality from the thinly painted fluorescent surfaces of the Day-Glo colors in the Moroccan series. The blue, blue-green, and gray, however, are epoxy enamels. Thus, the Irregular Polygons became the first pictures in which Stella risked juxtaposing pigments of differing characters. Especially in view of this, the control of the relative saturation of colors in *Conway I*, and the manner in which the contrasting hues were kept close in value, was exemplary. Stella had never previously "had much feeling for color-value gradation." But *Conway I*, he states,

is one of the first pictures in which I sort of let myself go with it. In that particular picture it seemed to work very well, and I was satisfied. But I didn't do much with it at the time; I just kept it in mind. Yet I think the Saskatchewan pictures [pages 148 and 150] are the fruition of that idea. The closeness of their values and their kind of general atmospheric haze seems to depend upon the same kind of color mentality or color instinct.

In executing the Irregular Polygons, Stella reserved thin unpainted strips that act as breathing spaces for the color fields by laying down ¼-inch masking tape between them. A cheap brand of tape was chosen so that the thinners of the paint would eat through it, giving the color areas a slightly irregular edge. These

117

breathing spaces had functioned in a similar way for the color bands of the Moroccan series—though the edges there were not irregular—but the larger shaped color masses of the 1966 Polygons made them even more imperative. "Without them," Stella observes,

Wolfeboro I. (1966)
Fluorescent alkyd and epoxy
paint on canvas, 13'4" x 8'4"

the Irregular Polygons would have become hard-edge paintings. Leaving them out would have killed the space, and made the pictures snap around a lot. It would have given them a kind of hard, brittle space, I'm almost sure. I was afraid of such a mechanical quality. They might have become too much like geometric drawing and like conventional geometric and hard-edge painting. I think what I had in mind in connection with these spaces was the example of Matisse—in something like the Red Studio. *It's perhaps an obvious device, but the necessity of separating the colors, that breathing, that soft line, and that identification of [color with] the ground seemed very important to me in those pictures.*

The facture—indeed the over-all conception of the Irregular Polygons—locates itself between that of Ellsworth Kelly and that of Kenneth Noland, the two painters of the post-Abstract Expressionist generation to whom Stella has at one time or another been closest (always excepting his Princeton friend, Darby Bannard). He met Kelly in December 1959 at The Museum of Modern Art, on the occasion of the opening of the exhibition *Sixteen Americans,* directed by Dorothy Miller, in which both were exhibiting. During the following year he was to be a frequent visitor at Kelly's studio at Coenties Slip. He admired Kelly's painting and was especially interested in certain early works which depended less on contoured shapes than did the pictures Kelly was exhibiting at the time. One of these was a monochrome yellow picture of rectangular format whose sole articulation was the slight literal projection forward of half of the surface—an effect achieved by the use of a deeper stretcher for that part. Kelly was pleased by Stella's interest and subsequently made a larger red version of the work. Kelly, in turn, was one of the few people to whom Stella showed the first sketches of the Irregular Polygons while he was pondering the shift in his style which these entailed; he was impressed with Kelly's encouragement.

Stella first saw Noland's painting at the latter's second show—largely Abstract Expressionist in spirit—at the Tibor de Nagy Gallery in 1958. He met Noland the following year at the time of the French & Co. exhibition in which Noland showed the first of his concentric circle paintings. Stella was extremely keen on this work, and during the period (1961–62) when Noland lived at the Chelsea Hotel in New York, the two saw a good deal of each other. Noland was, in turn, impressed by Stella's work, especially by the way in which the first shaped canvases held the wall as paintings instead of cutting themselves out as reliefs.

Moultonboro III. (1966)
Fluorescent alkyd and epoxy
paint on canvas, 9'2" x 10'¼"

One aspect of the Irregular Polygons that distinguishes them from Stella's earlier work is the degree to which their forms may be read as if they were moving in space, obliquely to the picture plane. This illusionism (which is not, however, of primary importance in the pictures), differs essentially from the illusionism of the Running V series. There, the simultaneous shift in light reflection and literal shape leaves the spectator no choice but to read a minimal recession or advance into the space of the pictures. But this illusion of a slight folding of the surface is a minor factor, and is subsumed into the prevailing two-dimensionality of those pictures. In the Irregular Polygons, on the other hand, nothing demands a spatial reading; it is a choice exercised by the spectator—in effect, a function of the way he approaches the pictures. When this option is exercised, however, and the pictures are read in illusionistic terms, oblique space becomes far more central to them than it had been in any of Stella's earlier work.

Michael Fried was the first to draw attention to, and emphasize, this spatial ambiguity. He noted, for example, that the trapezoid at the bottom of the Wolfeboro configuration (page 119) might be read as a rectangle seen in perspective.[93] In this respect, the parallelogram of *Conway I* might also suggest some oblique turning of a rectangle, and such a reading would, curiously enough, accord with the origin of the picture's motif. The original drawing was reversed top to bottom, and Stella is "almost positive that what I had in mind was a swinging mirror in my mother's bedroom. This was a rectangular mirror mounted on two pieces of wood with pivots."

Another example of possible illusionistic reading is demonstrated through a comparison of the Moultonboro and Chocorua configurations. The equilateral triangle of *Chocorua I* (page 113) demands to be read only as a frontal form situated, like its rectangle, in the picture plane. But while the red rectangle of *Moultonboro III* (page 120) is necessarily frontal, its yellow triangle, which presents itself as a frontal from, *might* also be read, as Fried observes, as turned obliquely from the picture plane.

That such optional spatial readings exist for most of the Irregular Polygons is unquestionable. How important these are to the understanding of the pictures, and how likely one is to visualize them is a matter of personal experience, taste, and context. Though considering the two-dimensional reading primary, Fried nevertheless makes a strong case for the complex ambiguities of the "extraordinary, and sheerly visual illusiveness" of these paintings. "This is not to say that, in a given picture, each shape seems to lie in a definite or specifiable depth-relation to every other," he wrote.

On the contrary, nothing is more fundamental to the nature of the new paint-

ings's illusiveness than the extreme ambiguity, indeterminacy and multivalence of the relations that appear to obtain among the individual shapes, as well as between those shapes and the surface of the picture (or, at any rate, the plane of that surface). . . . All this makes Stella's new paintings the most radically illusive and irreducibly ambiguous in the history of modernism.[94]

For Fried the bands of the Irregular Polygons, and in particular the mitering of their terminals, function especially to enhance the ambiguous illusionism:

In Moultonboro III, *for example, although one is not made to feel that the light yellow triangular band stands in any single or definite spatial relation to the turquoise blue Z-shaped band into which it fits, one nevertheless experiences their juxtaposition somewhat as though both were objects in the world, not simply nor even chiefly shapes on a flat surface—objects, moreover, whose relation to one another, and indeed whose actual character, are ineluctably ambiguous. This is most salient in the case of the Z-shaped turquoise band, largely because—or so it seems—its top and bottom segments are not parallel to one another. . . . That is, one tends to see the bottom segment, or the bottom two segments, as though somewhat from above and in perspective—while at the same time one is not given enough data to locate them in a definite spatial context, in relation either to contiguous shapes or to some ground plane. Moreover, because the top segment of the Z-form runs across the upper edge of the square and is therefore horizontal, one tends to experience that segment as frontal. But this would mean that the Z-form is not only irregular in two dimensions but bent or warped in three—though it is not at all clear which segment or segments are bent or warped and which, if any, are to be taken as normative. The bevelled ends of the Z-form, each parallel to nothing else in the painting, compound the ambiguity by implying that the respective planes of both the bottom and top segments are warped away from, or anyway are oblique to, that of the picture-surface—though, of course, they might* not *be. (Almost all the bands in Stella's new paintings are bevelled in this way—a brilliant stroke that adds immeasurably to the illusionistic power, and general complexity, of the paintings in question. . . .) The result is that the Z-form is seen as participating in a wide range of equally ambiguous and indeterminate spatial situations—more accurately, an* entire gamut *of such situations each of which is simultaneously not merely compatible with but continuous with or transparent to every other.*[95]

The illusionist potential of the Irregular Polygons is stressed even more strongly by Robert Rosenblum. For him,

the variety of acute and obtuse angles wrenches out of the flat color planes

Sanbornville I. (1966)
Fluorescent alkyd and epoxy
paint on canvas, 8'8" x 12'2"

122

strange perspective effects of oblique foreshortenings, of concave-convex ambiguities, all closely related to that new investigation of fictive depth on a plane surface . . . "Abstract Illusionism". . . .[96]

Union I. (1966)
Fluorescent alkyd and epoxy
paint on canvas, 8'8" x 14'6"

Rosenblum sees the illusionist potential of the Irregular Polygons as further enhanced by the juxtapositions of the matte and enamel surfaces of the fluorescent and epoxy paints and that of "icy and hot, tart and sweet hues, of shrilly contrasting tonal values."[97]

While Stella himself admits that the viewer may impute recession to various forms within the Irregular Polygons, his own reading plays down the potential stressed by Fried and Rosenblum, and he specifically rejects the association with Abstract Illusionism. Where Fried, for example, sees the mitered terminals of the bands as emphasizing the oblique illusiveness of the compositions, Stella thinks of them as establishing the cornering of flat planes. Indeed, their origin lay precisely in that function as it is illustrated within each of the mitered bands of such pictures as *Jasper's Dilemma* (page 77). "The paintings are pretty frontal," Stella observes. "I don't see twists in them. I want to see them flat. I see the planar ambiguities, but I minimize them as much as I can. I feel that this is the right way, the way I want to look at these pictures, and I feel that it is possible to do this without forcing oneself to see the paintings in a manner that really distorts them and their intentions."

Effingham I (page 110) illustrates a second group within the Irregular Polygons. Unlike *Chocorua I, Conway I,* and *Moultonboro III,* here only one of the two larger surface shapes—the diamond on the right—is a regular polygon. The orange field, which extends the upper left side of this diamond laterally and then swings diagonally upward to parallel it, contains elements of a parallelogram and a chevron but cannot be readily described. The vertical on the left—the only one in the composition—joins with the horizontal adjacent to it, forming a right angle that confers a degree of architectural stability upon the composition. The parallelogram at the top moves up from this; the diamond at the bottom, down from it. The support and balance of the configuration is precarious, however, and depends equally on the sense of being poised on the lower point of the diamond.

Unlike the situation in the pictures already discussed, the two main geometrical areas of *Effingham I* seem to abut rather than to interpenetrate each other. Their entire shapes, except for their common side, are given literally. Since the continuity of pattern that gave the other pictures unity depended in part on interpenetration, Stella was faced here with a different problem in making the com-

Moultonville I. (1966)
Fluorescent alkyd and epoxy
paint on canvas, 10'4" x 7'2"

position as a whole cohere. The solution lay in the special way in which the blue band was deployed. By carrying the latter for an extra turn within the yellow diamond, and by mitering it at that terminal, Stella at once diminished the intrinsic regularity and hence discreteness of the diamond shape. This made it more assimilable to the less regular geometry at its left—and provided a kind of meander pattern which, by continuing out of the diamond to embrace the orange area, pulled the two polygons of the composition together.

The Wolfeboro configuration (page 119) shares some of the characteristics of the Effingham paintings in that it is formed of two shapes that abut more than they interpenetrate. One is a regular trapezoid, the other, an irregular seven-sided area. Since the geometries of the first—or Chocorua—group were more predicated on interpenetration than juxtaposition, their constituent shapes involved a balance of depicted and literal definition. By comparison, the Effingham and Wolfeboro configurations depend less on depicted than on literal shaping.

The third—or Sanbornville—type of configuration, on the other hand, depends more on depicted than on literal shaping. Unlike any shape in the pictures thus far discussed, the depicted triangle on the left of *Sanbornville I* (page 123) is not implied—to say nothing of being necessitated—by anything in the literal silhouette of the picture, which it fails to penetrate. The resulting loss of a palpable reciprocity between the literal shape of the picture and the patterning within that shape explains what seems to me to be the partial failure of this configuration. In the absence of this governing reciprocity, the relative success or failure of the four Sanbornville paintings was more than ever a question of the color, functioning without the support that color had received from structure elsewhere in Stella's work.

The Irregular Polygons carried Stella into an area of openness, variety, and freedom of choice that resulted in a less steady level of success than was true of his earlier series. They range from some of his most daringly beautiful to his most unsatisfyingly overcomplicated pictures. Among the preparatory drawings for this series which he did not choose to use for paintings in 1966 were a few with circular motifs, which foretold aspects of the subsequent Protractor series (and Stella has contemplated returning to them for a new group of pictures). Indeed, the Irregular Polygons embodied such a great variety of pictorial ideas that Stella will probably find them a useful source of inspiration for years to come.

THE PROTRACTOR SERIES proper (not including the tangential Saskatchewan pictures), begun in 1967 and presently (October 1969) about three-quarters completed, is planned as a group of ninety-three pictures. Each of thirty-one

Ossipee I. (1966)
Fluorescent alkyd and epoxy
paint on canvas, 7'11" x 11'6"

different canvas formats (see diagrams, pages 136–37) is to be realized in three different designs, which Stella refers to as "interlaces," "rainbows," and "fans." Appropriately for these first of Stella's curvilinear compositions, most of the titles of the paintings are actually the names of ancient circular cities in Asia Minor; three bear the names of Islamic cities, and four have been given the names of the four gateways of the "round city" of Madinat as-Salam, i.e., Baghdad. (Stella had long been interested in Islamic art and traveled in the Near East in 1963). The city or gate of each title distinguishes the format—or literal shape—of the picture, while the Roman numeral following it designates the design group of its surface patterning.

Thus the format of *Darabjerd I* (page 130) is a full circle formed of two vertical protractors, the left of which is interlocked with a horizontal protractor shape. Each protractor-shaped area contains two concentric bands surrounding an inner field. In the area of interpenetration of the full and half circles—the area common to both—the bands interlace, and this lozenge-shaped conjunction is itself expanded by the addition of a band on each side which traverses an area not common to the two fields. In *Darabjerd II* (page 132) the same canvas format is divided into five individually framed sections filled with segments of concentric circular bands—the "rainbows." These arcs overlap in the area where the bands of *Darabjerd I* had interlaced—the square field in the lower center. In *Darabjerd III* (page 133) the same canvas format is articulated by substituting "fan"-shaped radial wedges for the circumference-echoing patterns of the previous two versions; here the transition in the crucial area where the full and half circles share a common surface is accomplished through a pattern formed by melding into continuous segments the wedges fanning out from the centers of both the full and the half circles.

Given the architectonic character of Stella's earlier work, it is not surprising that curvilinear—and, more particularly, circular—forms were banned from it. But since the circle is the simplest geometrical form—having even fewer co-ordinates than the square—it is understandable that an artist so concerned with concepts of both geometry and simplicity would eventually wish to confront it. Stella did not, to be sure, make use of discrete geometrical entities (such as the familiar polygons) at the outset. All the early pictures up to and including the Copper and Benjamin Moore series, whether shaped canvases or not, are involved essentially with variations on the right angle. Only in the polygons of the Purple series did Stella seem to have begun thinking primarily in such actual geometrical terms, a vocabulary he expanded in the Irregular Polygons. As we have just noted, the circle appeared for the first time in some of the drawings for this series.

Owing to their partial and occasionally wholly circular formats, the pictures of the Protractor series are, in the first instance, anti-tectonic in a way hitherto unknown in Stella's work. But they are also, paradoxically, the first that might be termed unremittingly architectural in both size and scale. From the Aluminum pictures to the Running V's, there was only an occasional canvas that exceeded 8 feet in either dimension. Even the Running V's, which generally extended laterally for 12 or 14 feet, were less than 8 feet high. The 24-foot long *De la nada Vida* that concluded that series was absolutely exceptional in Stella's work up to that date (1965), and this picture was itself less than 8 feet high. The Protractor pictures, on the other hand, are almost all wall size. The *smallest* dimension of the majority—those named after cities—is their 10-foot height. The widths average slightly less than 20 feet, the largest being that of *Madinat as-Salam,* which is 25 feet wide.

This new standard of quasi-architectural size is supported by a new set of scale relationships. Whereas the modular unit of the earlier pictures—their smallest interior measurement—was the 2½-inch width of the stripe, that of the interlace paintings is the 8-inch width of the bands (enlarged to 12 inches in those pictures named after city gates). To be sure, this monumentality and new sense of scale had been foreshadowed in the Irregular Polygons, where 8-inch bands made their first appearance. But the new scale of the Polygons was not quite matched by their size. Stella has rightly described their formats as "fairly compact"; their dimensions—vertical and horizontal—average only about 10 feet.

The Protractor series is architectural in still other respects. Though the dominant motifs are circular, every shape in the series—with the exception of the tondo—has a horizontal straight edge at the bottom of the composition. In the cases of the Sabra, Gur, Agbatana, and Kufa Gate formats there is, in addition, a vertical element forming a right-angle boundary to the shape. The Abra, Hagmatana, Takht-i-Sulayman, and Kufa Gate Shaped formats move even further in this direction, since both their left and their right sides as well as their bases may be construed as sides of a rectangle. The literal shape of the Kufa Gate Variation (see page 136) is the ultimate step in this development, since it consists of four overlapping protractor shapes, the base of which in each case forms one side of an absolutely square format.

The combination of the architectonic and the curvilinear is inherent, in this sense, in the very protractor motif on which this series is built, since the semicircle of the protractor rests firmly on its rectilinear base. This half circle—rather than the full circle—is the primary unit of all the formats. The simplest use of the unit—the Basra Gate format (which was one of the last to be painted)—is unique in the 16-inch width of its bands. It is also perhaps the most explicit

Darabjerd II. (1967). Polymer and fluorescent polymer paint on canvas, 10′ x 15′

Darabjerd III. (1967). Polymer and fluorescent polymer paint on canvas, 10′ x 15′

statement of the intrinsically architectural character of the series, suggesting, as it does, a great tunnel vault. Its 16-inch bands are literally the size of architectural supports. Indeed, even the somewhat narrower bands of the other interlace pictures in this series are still actually wide enough to stand for the piers and ribs of great vaulting systems, and in pictures like *Takht-i-Sulayman I* (page 139) these remind us in their complexity of the High Gothic. Writing of this picture Rosenblum observes that

the springing vaults of the arcs, some reaching as high as four feet above one's head, turn the painting into something that verges on the architectural, a work that might rest on the floor and be subject to natural physical laws of load and support. Seen on this immense scale, the thrusts and counterthrusts, the taut and perfect spanning of great spaces, the razor-sharp interlocking of points of stress all contrive to plunge the observer into a dizzying tour-de-force of aesthetic engineering.[98]

STELLA FOUND the idea for the first format in the series, that of the Sabra group, by simply turning his protractor at right angles to its initial position and placing its right tip where its left had been. He drew an outer band representing the boundary of the protractor and then paralleled it with a contiguous one inside. This left a protractor-shaped field within each pair of bands. *Sabra I* (page 142), which derives from this drawing, shows how the bands interlace in the area common to both protractor shapes. They are handled so as to bind the two protractor forms together without giving either one pre-eminence in the design. Both the brown and blue bands of the horizontal protractor cross *over* the black and *under* the red bands of the vertical protractor at the point where they meet near the tops of their arcs. But after having passed under the red band, the brown crosses over it in the left corner of the picture. By the same token, the blue band, which had passed over the black, sinks behind it in that same corner.

However complex these interweavings become (and they do so increasingly in other formats), they never produce illusions of receding space. This is due partly to their color having been applied flat and evenly, and partly to the fact that no band of one protractor group is ever consistently behind all those of another. Any band that might appear to be moving forward by virtue of overlapping another is soon pressed back by being overlapped itself—sometimes by the very band it had initially passed over. As in Pollock's webs, the drawing negates any tendency one might have to read the linear interpenetrations as definitions of receding space.

Among the most complex and beautifully realized interlace pictures are the 10 x 20-foot *Takht-i-Sulayman I* of 1967 (page 139) and *Hiraqla I* of 1968 (page 146). In the former, a full circle composed of two vertical protractors is framed tangentially on the left and right by vertical protractors. This sequence is locked together along the bottom by two horizontal protractors. In *Hiraqla I* the same vertical elements are recombined to form two full circles, linked this time by a single protractor serving as a base. Its fluorescent pinks, reds, oranges, yellows, and indigos give *Takht-i-Sulayman I* something of the air of psychedelic design—although, of course, in the form of high art. *Hiraqla I* has a more low-key and restrained palette, its cooler, paler salmons and light blues having been achieved by adding white to the fluorescent pigment.

In *Takht-i-Sulayman I* the interlace pattern is at its most complex. The segments of the overlapping bands vary enormously in length, and—in contrast to their treatment in certain other formats—no band is shown in its original, complete protractor form. (Nor, for that matter, are the pink, black, yellow, and green residual protractor shapes which, in the company of at least one of their surrounding bands, are presented integrally in such pictures as *Darabjerd I* [page 130] and *Hiraqla I*.)

As a result, *Takht-i-Sulayman I* contains nothing approaching a large field of a single color, in the sense that these existed in the Irregular Polygons. The spatial color of that series—the identification of a large field with a single hue—gives way to a sequence of accents in which the ribbons of color orchestrate the surface in terms of rhythmic variation rather than shaped masses. The constant mutations of hue, value, and saturation create intervallic relationships of a more decorative order than the structural massing of color in the Irregular Polygons. The distinct underlying geometrical structure of the latter pictures is here partly dissolved into a mosaic of colors, but it is a mosaic whose parallel lines serve as constant echoes of the framing edge.

To balance these decorative patterns with precisely the right intervallic leaps and pulsations Stella needed an especially wide and graduated range of color. Whereas, in his earlier work, he had almost exclusively used manufacturers colors, these no longer sufficed. Many of the new chromatic relationships depended upon colors mixed by Stella himself, sometimes in a combination of acrylic and fluorescent pigments.

Takht-i-Sulayman I was among the first Protractor paintings to be executed. Like other early pictures in the series, it had been preceded by a gouache sketch on graph paper, although here—as elsewhere—Stella changed his mind about the color in the course of making the actual painting. "After a while I stopped making these thorough color drawings," he reports, "because it was as much trouble to make them as it was to paint the picture." From time to time, when Stella found that a color was not working for him, he would repaint certain bands,

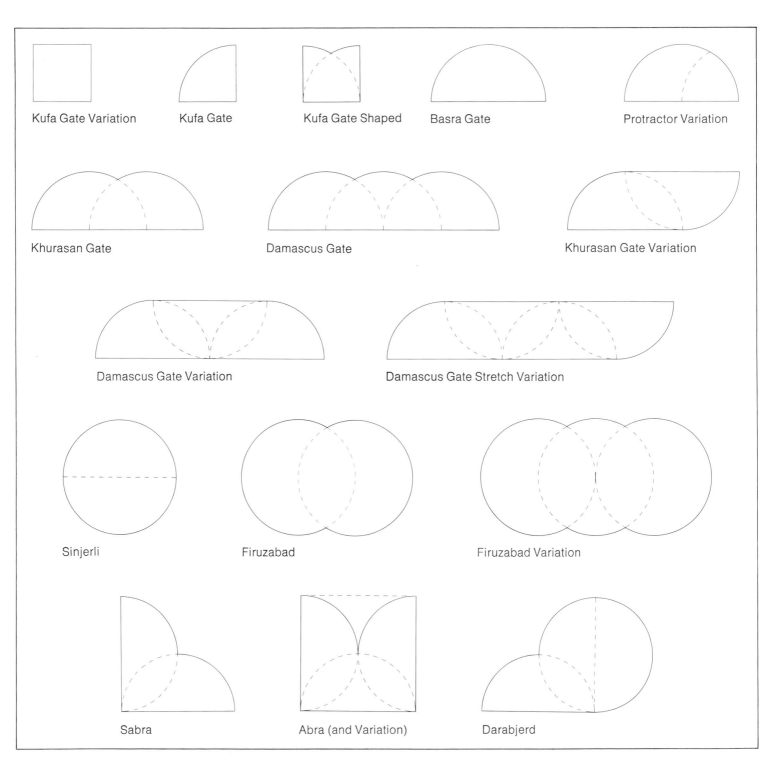

Kufa Gate Variation   Kufa Gate   Kufa Gate Shaped   Basra Gate   Protractor Variation

Khurasan Gate   Damascus Gate   Khurasan Gate Variation

Damascus Gate Variation   Damascus Gate Stretch Variation

Sinjerli   Firuzabad   Firuzabad Variation

Sabra   Abra (and Variation)   Darabjerd

136   Diagrammatic renderings of the 27 configurations of the Protractor series

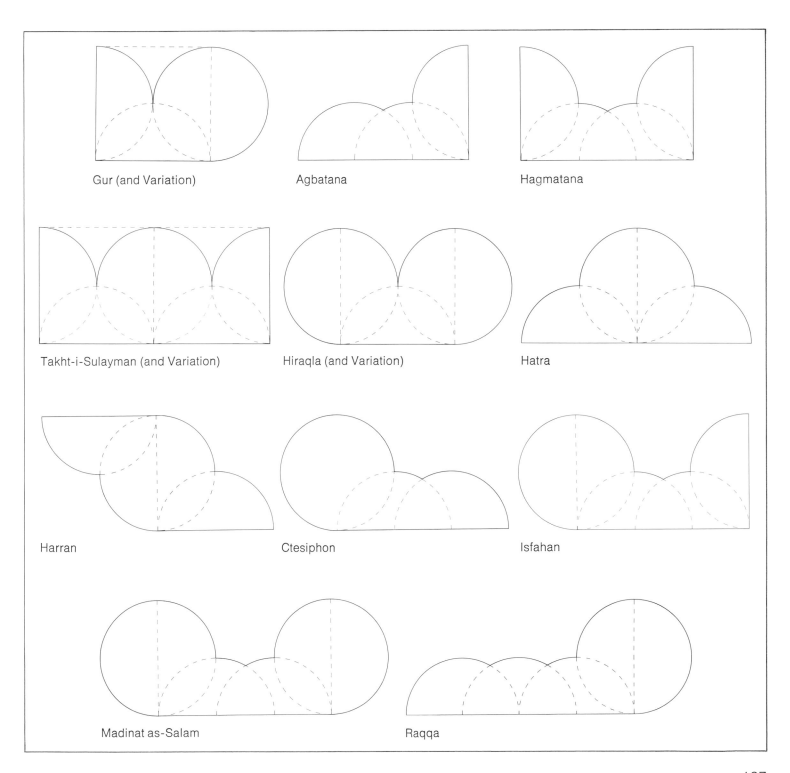

Gur (and Variation)

Agbatana

Hagmatana

Takht-i-Sulayman (and Variation)

Hiraqla (and Variation)

Hatra

Harran

Ctesiphon

Isfahan

Madinat as-Salam

Raqqa

137

but he did this as infrequently as possible because it tended to create a somewhat opaque paint film. Though the surfaces of the Protractor pictures are not quite as transparent as those of the Moroccan series (where no acrylics were mixed into the fluorescent colors), they have none of the density and weight characteristic of the Irregular Polygons. There, the fluorescent colors were generally given two or three coats and the enamels even more. The single coat that prevailed in the Protractor series gave the color a less substantial, slightly disembodied quality, which made it readily assimilable to the decorative patterning of these canvases.

Of the three design groups in the Protractor series, the interlace is by far the most interesting and the most successful. In a few instances, the rainbow version surpasses the interlace in the inventiveness of its color. But the rainbow layout is problematic. Its framing of the concentric arcs into areas of a quarter-circle cuts the total surface into autonomous sections that scan with much less coherence than either the interlaces or fans (compare *Darabjerd II,* page 132, with the other two versions of the format, pages 130 and 133).

At the same time, there is a strong contradictory tendency for the spectator's eye to complete the implied patterns of the rainbows' segmented arcs by connecting them to form circles. These meldings give the impression of taking place *under* the frames—which forces us to read the segmented arcs in their entirety as on a second plane in space. Stella did not intend the pictures to be read in this way; for him, the segmented arcs situate themselves in the same plane as their frames. But such is the force of the circular motif that we inevitably tend to complete it and, in so doing, are forced to see the circles behind the frames. This problem seems to me to be the inescapable flaw inherent in the rainbow configuration.

The more complicated the silhouette of the format, the more such difficulties plague the rainbows. It is not surprising, therefore, that the outstanding picture in the series should be the tondo. Here, in *Sinjerli II* (page 144), the consistent parallelism of the depicted arcs with the simple and powerful literal contour of the field—a phenomenon that does not obtain in the rainbows of any other format—makes it possible for the eye to overcome the divisive effects of the interior framing devices. This accomplished, the picture is free to succeed by virtue of its color.

The fan-design group does not seem to me to suffer from such inherent problems. At the same time, however, its radiating patterns denied Stella the structural force he had always derived from his frame-paralleling motifs. This force had allowed him a certain freedom in the layout of the interlaces; they

Takht-i-Sulayman I. (1967) Polymer and fluorescent polymer paint on canvas, 10′ x 20′

Agbatana II. (1968). Polymer and fluorescent polymer paint on canvas, 10' x 15'

Agbatana III. (1968). Polymer and fluorescent polymer paint on canvas, 10' x 15'

142

could be complicated precisely because they echoed and re-echoed the protractor shapes of the perimeter. The wedges of the fan patterns, however, while actually spreading from the bottom center of the protractor shape, are at the same time individually at varying angles to the contour of the field. This somewhat looser relationship of the parts in the fan pictures precluded the rhythmic vigor achieved in the interlaces through the reciprocity of literal and depicted shape. It nevertheless allowed for an interior continuity in the design that was not possible in the rainbows, especially in the areas where protractor shapes overlapped. Thus it is not surprising that the fan design led to successful solutions in those eccentric formats where the rainbow design was especially problematic. The design of *Agbatana III* (page 141), for example, assimilates the "bump" in the top of its profile much more successfully than does that of the rainbow version, *Agbatana II* (page 140).

The interlaces have no framing device as such. Inasmuch as the protractor contour of the literal shape is repeated throughout the surface, it does not assert itself as a specifically framing device. The rainbows have, as we have seen, many independent framing units within a single picture, and their visually disconcerting autonomy is reinforced by their individual colors. The fan pictures, on the contrary, have a single, unified framing device. This runs along the entire outer perimeter and continues into the center wedge of the fan pattern. In *Agbatana III,* for example, the saturated red of the framing device passes into the two wedges that are perpendicular to the bottom of the picture and the one perpendicular to its right side. This unbroken red area, traversing the surface as well as framing it, naturally sets the general condition of the color scheme for the whole picture. From this example it is easy to see why Stella almost always painted the framing elements of the fan pictures before determining the color of the wedges.

THE MARKEDLY DECORATIVE aspects of the interior patterning of the Protractor paintings were balanced by the strong structural concerns expressed in their field contours. This balance is most clearly demonstrated by the special unity of literal and depicted shapes achieved in the interlaces. However, in the summer of 1967, while on a visit to Canada, Stella began a group of pictures on regular rectangular formats, which signaled a new and more sweeping commitment to decorative patterning and to color as over and against structure. In this still-evolving Saskatchewan series, the particular kind of reciprocal relationship between surface pattern and canvas shape that previously characterized Stella's painting has been significantly altered. Stella had, of course, painted square and rectangular pictures in the years following the inception of "shaped canvas"

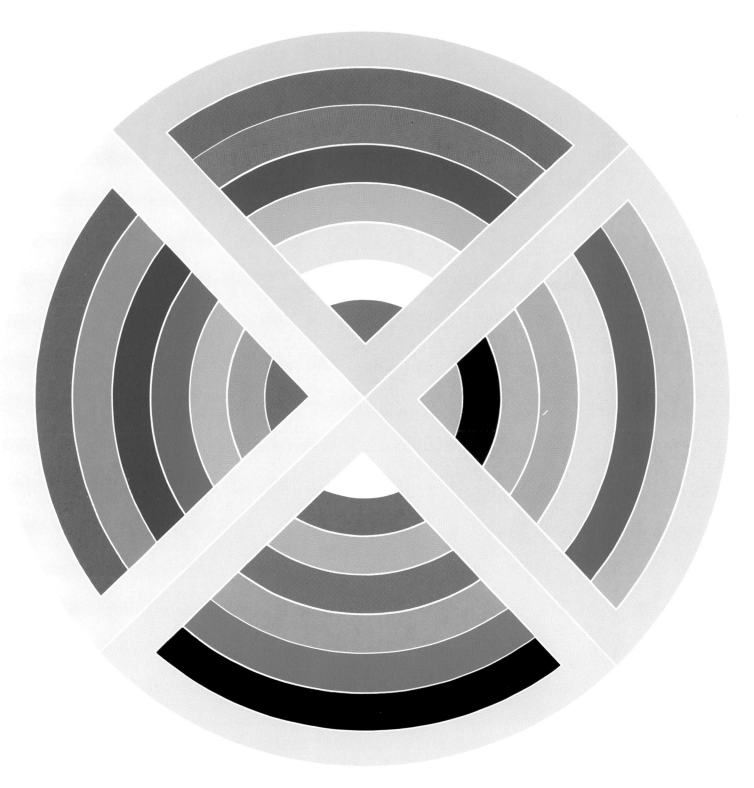

144

(notably the Benjamin Moore and Moroccan series), but in all these pictures the literal forms followed from the geometrically regular depicted patterns. In pictures such as *Saskatoon I* of 1968 (page 148) and *Flin Flon III* of 1969 (page 150), however, the depicted shapes are semicircular, and yet these semicircular units are never allowed to function as segments of the framing edge (as they had done in the Protractor series). Instead, they are framed by the squares and rectangles that now constitute the basic shapes of the canvases.

To be sure, the straight edges or sides of the Saskatchewan pictures still function as the bases of protractor shapes. In that sense, the Saskatchewan group represents an offshoot of the Protractor series (particularly of the square Kufa Gate configurations). But what distinguishes them from the Protractor pictures, and indeed, from all Stella's earlier work, is the introduction of figure-ground relationships. The lime-green ground of *Saskatoon I* fills areas on the top, bottom, and sides of the picture—areas that might earlier have been literally cut away. It also reappears in the center of the picture where one would have expected (following the model of the Protractor series) an interlacing of bands. It is true, of course, that the new regular formats were in part necessitated by the fact that Stella found it impossible to have shaped stretchers made for him in Canada. But the innovation of this series—the new figure-ground relationship—could have been avoided even in these regular formats if Stella had simply filled out the protractor patterns (as he had in fact done in *Kufa Gate*).

Instead, he chose to truncate many of the bands at their point of intersection, and the resulting arabesque pattern seems not so much to derive from the protractor as it constitutes a new kind of centralized four-petaled motif. Moreover, the floral connotations of this design are reinforced by decorative pastel colors that are all held in relatively close value relationships (a handling of color first attempted by Stella in *Conway I;* see above, pp. 114–17). The earliest of the Protractor pictures, those of 1967, had involved large intervals of value and saturation, as in *Takht-i-Sulayman I* (page 139). In the course of 1968, however, Stella narrowed these extremes and, in the process, dropped the use of black. The lime-green ground of *Saskatoon I* and the salmon ground of *Flin Flon III* act as mediators between hues that are never markedly darker or lighter, warmer or cooler, than they themselves.

Unlike the conventional relationship between figure and ground, the ground here does not constitute a foil for the figure. Rather, it is itself entirely contoured by the arabesque vocabulary of the figure. The scalloped interior contours and straight edges of the grounds tie them into an immediate rhythmic relationship with the arcs and straight edges of the floral motif. The petals of the floral design, in turn, reach out to touch all four corners of the field, tightly locking the

ensemble together. This limited conception of a figure-ground relationship, by avoiding the contrasts or polarities that such relationships normally create, is paralleled by Stella's limitation of the color to a very narrow value range. Taken together, these two aspects endow the Saskatchewan pictures with a counterpart—in the context of color and arabesque—of the synoptic unity Stella had earlier achieved in the context of rigorous structure and monochromy.

GIVEN STELLA'S INTEREST in Hiberno-Saxon illumination and Islamic art, it is not surprising that these styles (as well as Orphic Cubism and 1930s ''moderne'') should have been invoked in discussions of his recent work, particularly in connection with the interlace and rainbow pictures. (Rosenblum has drawn an interesting analogy between the Protractor pictures and the interior of the Radio City Music Hall.[99]) Stella himself sees the work of Delaunay as being the most important of these influences, although he only became aware of the relationship to Orphism after the series was underway; he doubts that the 1930s period style would have been discussed at all were it not for the recent work of Lichtenstein. More influential than any of these styles, however, has been the painting of

Hiraqla I. (1968)
Polymer and fluorescent polymer paint on canvas, 10′ x 20′

opposite
Sinjerli III. (1967)
Polymer and fluorescent polymer paint on canvas, diameter 10′

146

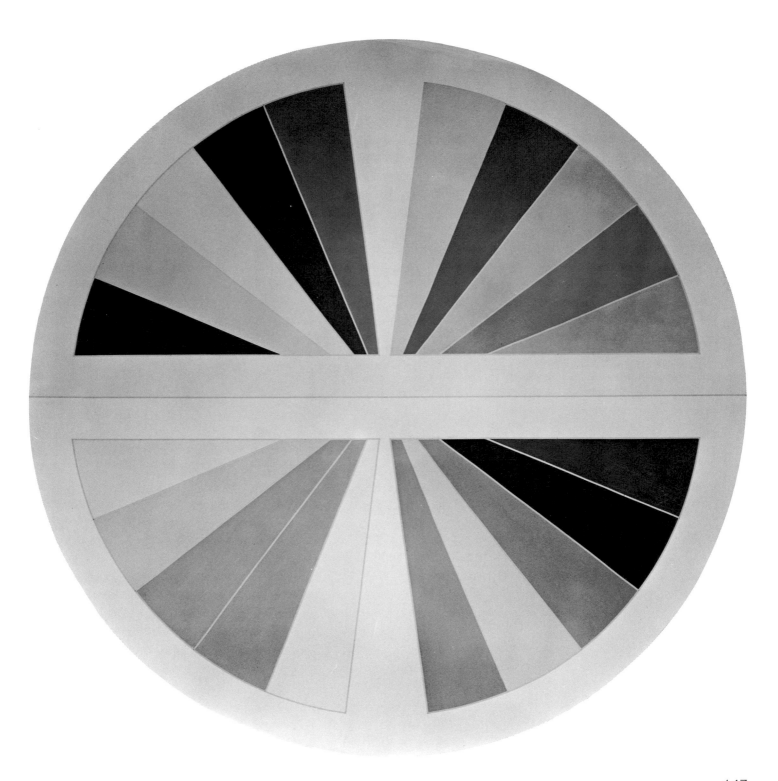

Saskatoon I. (1968)
Polymer and fluorescent
polymer paint on canvas,
8' x 16'

Matisse. It is primarily under *his* star that Stella's enterprise has evolved in recent years. It is Matisse whom he has looked at hardest, and it is Matisse's conception of a decorative high art that has most stimulated him. "There are some overtones of Orphic Cubism that get into the pictures as a result of the sheer geometry of the protractor," Stella observes,

and while there's no getting around that, I think that these relationships are visually incidental in that they do not essentially determine the character of the pictures. Or undermine it, certainly . . . My main interest has been to make what is popularly called decorative painting truly viable in unequivocal abstract terms. Decorative, that is, in a good sense, in the sense that it is applied to Matisse. What I mean is that I would like to combine the abandon and indulgence of Matisse's Dance *with the over-all strength and sheer formal inspiration of a picture like his* Moroccans. *Matisse himself seems to have tried it in the* Bathers by a River, *and that's as close as he seems to me to have come. Maybe this is beyond abstract painting. I don't know, but that's where I'd like my painting to go.*

Anyway, it seems to me that at their best, my recent paintings are so strongly involved with pictorial problems and pictorial concerns that they're not conventionally decorative in any way.

THIS PRESENTATION of Stella's work spans slightly more than one decade. When Stella's Black paintings first appeared, they seemed to many to have come virtually from nowhere, to have no stylistic heritage, and to represent a rejection of everything that painting seemed to be. Increasingly over the years these pictures—and Stella's subsequent work—have revealed their deep and manifold roots in the tradition of modern painting.

In a period in which abstract painting has been frequently marked by the narrowness of its stylistic and conceptual range, Stella's variety has been breathtaking. Moreover, he has achieved it through a willingness to risk and suffer failure in a manner that few painters have the courage to do. His variety is, of course, more than merely technical or stylistic; it embraces an immense gamut of feeling. The range that separates his paintings of the beginning of the decade from those of the end is characterized by the span between the elusive light of the Black, Aluminum, and Copper pictures and the brilliant and sensuous color of the more recent work, and by the constant tension between those expressive elements and the controlled geometrical drawing that orders them. Stella is now only thirty-three years old, an age at which many major painters have not yet found their mature styles. His endurance faces many challenges, not the least of which is the quality of his own past.

149

Flin Flon III. (1969). Polymer and fluorescent polymer paint on canvas, 8' x 8'

Notes

All comments by Stella for which no source is given are from conversations with the author taped in June and September of 1969 and subsequently edited by the artist.

1   From the unpublished transcript of taped interviews made in 1966 for a program in the series "U.S.A. Artists" produced by Lane Slate for National Educational Television. Stella was interviewed by Alan Solomon, but the latter's questions are not included throughout the transcript, which is in the files of NET, New York. Only a small part of the material was actually used in the program. As with all other quotations of extemporaneous remarks by Stella that appear in this book, they have been edited by him.

2   *Ibid.*

3   *Ibid.*

4   *Ibid.*

5   *Ibid.*

6   *Ibid.*

7   *Ibid.*

8   *Ibid.*

9   *Ibid.*

10   Motherwell's work was first drawn to Stella's attention by Darby Bannard. Stella studied Motherwell's *The Voyage* at The Museum of Modern Art quite carefully, and he was also especially interested in the collage *Pancho Villa, Dead and Alive.* Later, at the time of the Motherwell retrospective at The Museum of Modern Art in 1965, he was struck by *The Little Spanish Prison* (1941–44), a stark composition of vertical bands set off by a black rectangle. (This rectangle had originally been magenta, but in 1944 Motherwell painted it black; in 1969 he decided to remove this black, which was covering the magenta when Stella first saw the picture.)

   Although Stella had a high opinion of Motherwell's *"Je t'aime"* paintings, he was put off by what he considered the romantic pretentiousness of the French inscriptions painted across the surfaces of the paintings. In his parody of the series, Stella inscribed such titles as *"Your lips are blue"* and *"Mary Lou douches with pine-scented Lysol."*

11   NET transcript; see above, note 1.

12   *Ibid.*

13   This unique aspect of Johns's work was first noted in my "Younger American Painters," *Art International* (Zurich),
Jan. 1960, p. 26. The complexity of Johns's work in this respect was subsequently elaborated in the refined analysis of Leo Steinberg in "Jasper Johns," *Metro* (Milan), no. 415, 1961, pp. 90–109 (reprinted as *Jasper Johns* [New York, 1963]).

14   NET transcript; see above, note 1.

15   See Thomas B. Hess, *Willem de Kooning* (New York, 1968), pp. 22–24.

16   Barbara Rose has indicated to me that the deep stretchers were Darby Bannard's idea, and that he and Stella had begun making stretchers that way while still at Princeton.

   Most of Stella's stretchers are slightly less than 3 inches deep inasmuch as the size at which lumber yards have been allowed by their trade associations to cut 1x3's has diminished over the years to approximately 13/16 x 2-5/8". The exact depth of the stretcher is not an issue since, in spite of assertions to the contrary, Stella has never considered it a function of the module of the surface pattern.

17   Stella had an arrangement with a painter named J. Huriash who lived in Astoria, Queens. As Huriash worked for unusually low rates, he got many jobs in the slum districts where the courts were forcing landlords to repaint. The ambiance of these jobs is directly connected with the titles of the Black pictures.

18   NET transcript; see above, note 1.

19   *Ibid.*

20   This letter to the editor, dated February 1, 1961, actually written by Hollis Frampton, was not published. A copy of it is in the artist's file at The Museum of Modern Art.

21   Graph-paper drawings of the configurations of some of the Black pictures do exist but, like many such drawings of the early pictures, they were executed some years after the paintings.

22   The lecture, delivered sometime during January or February, is included as an appendix in Robert Rosenblum's monograph, *Frank Stella,* to be published by Penguin Books (Penguin New Art, 1), 1970.

23   Stella believes that what he had in mind in regard to symmetry was the discussion of harmony in C. K. Ogden and I. A. Richards, *The Meaning of Meaning,* 1st ed. (New York, 1923); 8th ed. (New York, 1946). He was introduced to the book by Patrick Morgan.

24   What Stella had in mind here were the flat and opaque areas of single colors in Darby Bannard's painting of that time.

25   Stella would now amend this sentence to read "forces *deep* illusionistic space out of the painting . . ."

26 "I was trying to find out," he now says in elaborating on the lecture, "whether abstract painting, or at least abstract figuration, could have its own space—one that it didn't share with representational painting or figuration."

27 From an interview by Bruce Glaser with Stella and Donald Judd broadcast by WBAI-FM, New York, February 1964, under the title "New Nihilism or New Art?"; published as "Questions to Stella and Judd," ed. by Lucy R. Lippard, *Art News* (New York), Sept. 1966, pp. 55–61. Hereafter, all remarks from this interview will refer to the *Art News* publication.

28 The closure on the right and the compensatory balances related to a left-right scanning obtained in iconic as well as narrative Renaissance painting. See Heinrich Wölfflin's comparison of Raphael's *Sistine Madonna* in its correct and a reversed form in his classic exposition of the problem, "Über das Rechts und Links im Bilde," in *Gedanken zur Kunstgeschichte* (Basel, 1940), pp. 82–83.

29 For a more extensive discussion of this aspect of Cézanne's aesthetic, see the author's "Jackson Pollock and the Modern Tradition, V. Cubism and the Later Evolution of the All-Over Style," *Artforum* (Los Angeles), Apr. 1967, pp. 23–24.

30 I have in mind here particularly the "checkerboard" compositions and the equilateral diamonds.

31 "Questions to Stella and Judd," *op. cit.,* p. 55.

32 Compensatory balance, which contains and derives from the question of left-to-right scanning, constitutes, as Rudolph Arnheim observed, "a knotty problem" (see his *Art and Visual Perception* [Berkeley, 1954], pp. 18–19). Neither Gestalt psychologists nor physiologists have offered convincing explanations for the prevalence of the left-right reading. In the history of Western art it seems probable that this tendency has followed from the practice of reading texts and has hence been strongest where the art has been most dominated by narrative conventions. As modern painting has been decidedly non-narrative in character, it is quite natural that it should have progressively challenged the inherited narrative mode of reading pictures, and that this challenge—like the one directed against the conventions for reading fictive deep space into pictures—should increase in proportion to abstractness.

33 See, for example, Clement Greenberg, "Modernist Painting," *Art and Literature* (Lausanne), Spring 1965, p. 198; article reprinted with non-substantive changes in Gregory Battcock (ed.), *The New Art: A Critical Anthology* (New York, 1966), pp. 101–10.

34 Robert Coates, "Art," *New Yorker,* Jan. 2, 1960, pp. 60–61.

35 Max Kozloff, "Art," *Nation* (New York), Apr. 21, 1962, pp. 364–66.

36 There are two alternative spatial readings for the classic configuration of Pollock. Since none of the conventional visual cues for what we call illusionistic space are present, we are *required* to see only the very shallow space created by the actual displacement of the overlapping skeins, whose unique anti-sculptural line implies no space in itself (see the author's "Jackson Pollock and the Modern Tradition, II. The All-Over Compositions and the Drip Technique," *Artforum* [Los Angeles], Feb. 1967, pp. 20–21). The skeins are seen suspended in front of the ground of the bare canvas or, alternatively, in front of a painted ground which—most importantly—is applied with an absolute evenness that precludes any pressure to read its surface as other than flat. The primary reading is that which locates Pollock's web in a shallow frontal space, i.e., the image floating in front of a finite ground. This space—as indeed the entire all-over structure of which it is a part—was distilled, at a considerable remove, from Analytic Cubism, but it had been drained of all tactile sculptural space. However, since an otherwise uncued color area does not *necessarily* assert itself as flat, the grounds may also be read as "infinite" in their spatial suggestion. Such a spatial reading, favored by certain critics, is in effect an option taken up by the spectator and, unlike all earlier illusionist space in painting, is not dictated by the picture itself. For the purposes of the present discussion, it is of no importance whether Pollock's space is said to be shallow or infinite, so long as its depth is considered approximately even throughout.

37 NET transcript; see above, note 1.

38 By the middle sixties the radicalism of Pollock's enterprise was widely felt among artists whose styles, at first glance, seemed totally unrelated. "Several times," wrote Barbara Rose, "in the course of the series of panels 'The Critic's Colloquium' held at N.Y.U. in 1966–67, younger artists such as Stella and Judd stated or implied that the break represented by Pollock's all-over paintings represented a caesura as significant and radical as Manet's break with the Academy" (*A New Aesthetic,* catalogue of an exhibition held at the Washington Gallery of Modern Art, Washington, D.C., May 6–June 25, 1967, p. 20 note 20).

39 See the author's "Jackson Pollock and the Modern Tradition, V. Cubism and the Later Evolution of the All-Over Style," *Artforum* (Los Angeles), Apr. 1967, pp. 18–31.

40 *Ibid.*

41 Michael Fried, "Shape as Form: Frank Stella's New Paintings," in *Frank Stella. An Exhibition of Recent Paintings,* Pasadena Art Museum, October 18–November 20, 1966, p. 6; reprinted in *Artforum* (Los Angeles), Nov. 1966, pp. 18–27, and in a somewhat revised version in Henry Geldzahler, *New York Painting and Sculpture: 1940–1970,* catalogue of an exhibition held at The Metropolitan Museum of Art, New York, October 18, 1969–February 1, 1970, pp. 403–25. Hereafter, references to Fried's essay will be to the *Artforum* publication.

42 NET transcript; see above, note 2. Elsewhere in the same discussion with Alan Solomon, Stella rightly took exception to the widespread assumption that the simplicity of his design conceptions—a quantitative factor—automatically precluded high quality. "I don't think that the fact that they are easy to see," he said, "means that they are lesser in quality . . . than other paintings which have a more complicated organization."

43 "Questions to Stella and Judd," *op. cit.,* p. 59.

44 Hilton Kramer, "Frank Stella: 'What You See Is What You See,'" *New York Times,* Dec. 10, 1967, sec. 2, p. 39.

45 Brian O'Doherty, "Frank Stella and a Crisis of Nothingness," *New York Times,* Jan. 19, 1964, sec. 2, p. 21.

46 Max Kozloff, "Frank Stella and Kenneth Noland, I," *Nation* (New York), Mar. 28, 1966, pp. 370–72; reprinted in Max Kozloff, *Renderings* (New York, 1968), pp. 264–69.

47 Though the degree of each painter's contribution to the ever-evolving vocabulary of painting differs, I venture to say that there has not been a single great artist in the last hundred years who has not made an important contribution to the *plastic* adventure of modern art.

48 NET transcript; see above, note 1.

49 "Questions to Stella and Judd," *op. cit.,* p. 60.

50 *Three American Painters,* catalogue of an exhibition held at the Fogg Art Museum, Harvard University, April 21–May 30, 1965, p. 44.

51 "Recentness of Sculpture," in Maurice Tuchman (ed.), *American Sculpture of the Sixties,* catalogue of an exhibition held at the Los Angeles County Museum of Art, April 28–June 25, 1967, p. 26.

52 "After Abstract Expressionism," *Art International* (Zurich), Oct. 1962, p. 29.

53 "Jackson Pollock and the Modern Tradition, I. The Myths and the Paintings," *Artforum* (Los Angeles), Feb. 1967, p. 14.

54 In "The Ides of Art: The Attitudes of 10 Artists on Their Art and Contemporaneousness," *Tiger's Eye* (Westport, Conn.), Dec. 1947, p. 44.

55 "Questions to Stella and Judd," *op. cit.,* pp. 58–59.

56 "Younger American Painters," *op. cit.,* p. 25.

57 Letter dated October 28, 1960, recommending Stella for a Fulbright grant; carbon copy in the artist's file at The Museum of Modern Art.

58 From an extended discussion of the Black pictures in Rosenblum, *op. cit.,* p. 18. The first full-scale magazine article on Stella's work was written by Rosenblum, "Frank Stella. Five Years of Variations on an 'Irreducible' Theme," *Artforum* (San Francisco), Mar. 1965, pp. 20–25.

59 The phrase "die Fahne hoch" is from the *Horst Wessel Lied,* which was often heard in the sound tracks of the Nuremberg rallies. Stella does not recall seeing the Leni Riefenstahl films but is sure that he has seen much of their footage in documentaries.

60 "The Fascist architects," Stella notes, "wanted to get on firm foundations. And the irony of their using what was considered to be classical art struck me . . . as did the whole concept of public buildings in the U.S.A.—which amount to much the same kind of thing."

61 Stella speculates as to whether there is not some relationship between quality in art and architecture and the will to impose it—a kind of "totalitarianism of quality." He sees this essentially as a problem: "the interaction of aesthetic quality and control, both on the viewer and on oneself."

62 NET transcript; see above, note 1.

63 *Ibid.*

64 Philip Johnson Collection, New Canaan, Conn.

65 "Shape as Form," *op. cit.,* p. 18.

66 *Three American Painters, op. cit.*

67 *Ibid.,* p. 23.

68 *Ibid.,* p. 40.

69 *Ibid.*

70 "Shape as Form," *op. cit.*

71 *Ibid.,* p. 18.

72 *Ibid.,* p. 19.

73 *Ibid.,* p. 18; italics mine.

74 *Three American Painters, op. cit.,* p. 40; italics mine.

75 See Barbara Rose, *A New Aesthetic, op. cit.,* p. 18 note 6, paragraph 2.

76 *Three American Painters, op. cit.,* p. 40.

77 See above, p. 12 and note 13. John Coplans (*Serial Imagery,* catalogue of an exhibition held at the Pasadena Art Museum, September 17–October 27, 1968, p. 98) also stresses this relationship: "Stella maintains a one-to-one relationship between the emblem and the overall shape of the canvas. His emblematicism, then, is somewhat similar to Jasper John's [*sic*] rendition of the American Flag."

77a *Jules Olitski. Paintings 1963–1967,* catalogue of an exhibition held at The Corcoran Gallery of Art, Washington, D.C., April 28–June 11, 1967, p. 8.

77b *Ibid.,* pp. 21–22 note 13.

77c Hilton Kramer, "Representative of the 1960's," *New York Times,* Mar. 20, 1966, sec. 2, p. 21.

78 Five of the six paintings in the Copper series were executed in the spring of 1960 but were severely damaged by exposure in Stella's studio. The definitive versions of these five—plus the sole version of *Creede*—were painted on new canvases in 1961. I have therefore used the dating 1960–61 for all these pictures except *Creede.*

79 The earlier, damaged version of *Ouray* has since been restored and is in the collection of the artist. The other version (1963) is in a private collection in New York.

80 "Questions to Stella and Judd," *op. cit.,* p. 58.

81 NET transcript; see above, note 2.

82 These pictures have been referred to as "magenta" (Fried) and "lavender" (Rosenblum), but they should be called purple, not simply because that was their hue, but because this hue was consciously chosen from the range of six primaries and secondaries, the methodically limited color scheme Stella used through that date. As the pictures faded some of them began to look lavender, but none have ever looked magenta.

83 *Op. cit.,* p. 27.

84 Collection Mr. and Mrs. Gilbert F. Carpenter, Greensboro, North Carolina.

85 *Op. cit.,* p. 39.

86 *Ibid.,* pp. 36–39.

87 *Ibid.,* p. 36.

88 *Ibid.,* p. 39.

89 Reproduced in Geldzahler, *op. cit.,* p. 319. Barbara Rose has communicated to me some interesting comments about the painting and its title: "*Sangre de Cristo . . .* is the last in the series of the Copper paintings, all of which were named after towns in the San Juan Mountains of Colorado. Sangre de Cristo is a mountain range to the east of it. [The painting] was conceived long before it was executed and was meant as the coda of the series."

90 NET transcript; see above, note 1.

91 "Shape as Form," *op. cit.,* p. 18.

92 The original *Effingham I,* painted in 1966 as were the other works in this series, was irreparably damaged while being moved from Stella's studio. In 1967 he executed a new picture in the Effingham format but with different colors. Thus, this was actually the fifth Effingham painting, but Stella chose to give it the title of the destroyed painting.

93 "Shape as Form," *op. cit.,* p. 23.

94 *Ibid.,* p. 24.

95 *Loc. cit.*

96 *Op. cit.,* p. 44. Rosenblum characterizes Abstract Illusionism by referring to it as a movement "which Barbara Rose has found a vital current in much painting of the 1960s, from Miriam Schapiro and Larry Zox to Ron Davis and Darby Bannard." In her article ("Abstract Illusionism," *Artforum* [New York], Oct. 1967, pp. 33–37), Miss Rose was not concerned with Stella's work as such but with the general problem of reconciling illusionism with flatness.

97 *Op. cit.,* p. 45.

98 *Ibid.,* pp. 48–49.

99 *Ibid.,* p. 50.

Chronology

1936

May 12. Frank Philip Stella born in Malden, Massachusetts, a suburb of Boston, to Frank and Constance Aida Santonelli Stella. Father a gynecologist, mother had attended art school.

1950–54

Attends Phillips Academy, Andover. Studies with abstract painter Patrick Morgan and is encouraged by both Morgan and his wife, the painter Maud Morgan. Sees paintings by Arthur Dove and Hans Hofmann in the Morgans' collection. Meets Carl Andre and Hollis Frampton.

1954–58

1954. Enters Princeton University.
1955. Studies history and attends William Seitz's open painting-studio, attended also by Darby Bannard. Begins to visit museums and galleries in New York City frequently.
1956. Studies painting with Stephen Greene, artist-in-residence. Meets Michael Fried, also a student at Princeton.
1957. Is influenced by Abstract Expressionism. Designs covers for college literary magazine *Nassau Lit*. Is introduced by Stephen Greene to Emile de Antonio [now a documentary film-maker]. Writes junior year essay on Hiberno-Saxon manuscripts. From members of Art Department faculty begins to hear about work of Jasper Johns.
1958. January-February: At the Leo Castelli Gallery sees Flag and Target paintings for first time in Johns's first one-man exhibition. Spring: During last months at Princeton paints a number of works influenced by Rothko and Gottlieb in contrast to earlier de Kooning- and Frankenthaler-influenced paintings. Graduates with A.B. degree in history.
Summer: Moves to New York City; occupies storefront studio on Eldridge Street on Lower East Side. Begins "transitional" paintings.
Fall: Works as house painter three or four days a week. Moves to loft on West Broadway. Emile de Antonio brings Eleanor Ward of Stable Gallery down to studio.
Winter: Is introduced by Darby Bannard to art critic Clement Greenberg. Begins Black series. Titles of "transitional" and Black paintings—e.g., *Astoria, Tomlinson Court Park, Arundel Castle*—refer to buildings and places in New York that have personal associations. Begins seeing Carl Andre and Hollis Frampton again.

1959

Continues Black series.
March. Sees work of Barnett Newman for first time at exhibition at French & Co.
Art historian Jerome Rothlein urges John Myers of Tibor de Nagy Gallery to look at Stella's work.
April 7–25. Exhibits professionally for first time: *Club Onyx,* painting from Black series, included in exhibition *Selections* at the Tibor de Nagy Gallery. Dorothy Miller, Curator of Museum Collections at The Museum of Modern Art, having heard of work from William Seitz, visits exhibition.
Spring. William Seitz recommends work to Charles Parkhurst, Director of Allen Memorial Art Museum at Oberlin College, who is organizing an exhibition of young American talent.
May 11–30. *Luncheon on the Grass* (1958), *Our Lady of Perpetual Help I* [later titled *Club Onyx*] (1959), *Our Lady of Perpetual Help II* [later titled *Seven Steps*] (1959), and *Bethlehem's Hospital* (1959), all "transitional" paintings, included in exhibition *Three Young Americans* at Allen Memorial Art Museum. Unsigned text accompanying Stella's listing in catalogue is by Carl Andre.
June. Is introduced by Princeton art historian Robert Rosenblum to Jasper Johns and Robert Rauschenberg.
Summer. Dorothy Miller, organizing *Sixteen Americans* exhibition, visits studio accompanied by Leo Castelli who has planned his own visit at the suggestion of Robert Rosenblum. Miss Miller returns for second visit with Alfred Barr, Director of Museum Collections at The Museum of Modern Art, who also responds enthusiastically to work. Miss Miller invites Stella to participate in exhibition.
August. Joins the Leo Castelli Gallery.
Fall. Exhibition at the Malden Public Library of paintings shown at Allen Memorial Art Museum.
October 6–17. *Clinton Plaza,* painting from Black series, included in exhibition *Opening of the New Gallery* at the Leo Castelli Gallery; becomes first painting to be sold outside immediate circle of friends. William Rubin, art historian teaching at Sarah Lawrence College, sees exhibition, makes first of periodic visits to studio.
November. At French & Co. meets Kenneth Noland at Noland's first exhibition of concentric circle paintings.
Is introduced by Carl Andre to Barbara Rose, graduate student of art history at Columbia University.
E. C. Goossen, teaching art history and criticism and Director of Exhibitions at Bennington College, Vermont, visits studio and likes work.
December 9–January 7. *Jill,* from Black series, shown at *Metropolitan Young Artists Show* at National Arts Club, New York, an exhibition of younger artists selected by older artists, for which Stella is chosen by Adolph Gottlieb.
December 16–February 14. *"Die Fahne hoch,"* Tomlinson Court

Park, The Marriage of Reason and Squalor, and *Arundel Castle* (all 1959) shown in *Sixteen Americans,* exhibition directed by Dorothy Miller at The Museum of Modern Art. Catalogue contains slightly revised version of Carl Andre statement in Oberlin catalogue. First newspaper and magazine criticism of Stella's work; numerous unfavorable reviews (bibl. 62) and 1 favorable (bibl. 38). Meets Ellsworth Kelly.

December 27. In letter, "An Artist Writes To Correct and Explain," published in *New York Herald Tribune* replies to unfavorable criticism by newspaper's art critic.

December 30. *The Marriage of Reason and Squalor* acquired by The Museum of Modern Art; first museum purchase.

1960

January–February. With some of the other artists in *Sixteen Americans* exhibition participates in panel discussion at New York University. Delivers lecture to students at Pratt Institute.

Completes Black series. Begins Aluminum series, paints first shaped canvases. Titles—e.g., *Luis Miguel Dominguín, Avicenna, Newstead Abbey*—are names of matadors, Arabic philosophers, famous places, etc.

May 3–31. *Tomlinson Court Park* included in exhibition *New American Painting* at Galerie Neufville [later Galerie Lawrence], Paris, in which work by Youngerman, Kelly, Bluhm, Louis, Noland, Parker, Sanders, Jenkins, Rauschenberg, and Stankiewicz also shown.

Summer. Begins Copper series. Titles—e.g., *Ouray, Creede*—are names of towns in San Juan Mountains, Colorado. Paintings damaged by exposure.

September 27–October 15. First one-man exhibition at the Leo Castelli Gallery; work from Aluminum series shown.

October. Applies for Fulbright grant to study in Japan; Alfred Barr and Dorothy Miller, among others, write letters of recommendation. Meets Donald Judd.

December 19–February 12. *The Marriage of Reason and Squalor* shown in exhibition *Recent Acquisitions* at The Museum of Modern Art.

1961

March. Travels in Florida with Sidney Guberman. Visits Florida Southern College in Lakeland to see buildings of Frank Lloyd Wright, is especially impressed with the Memorial Chapel. Fulbright grant refused.

Repaints Copper series damaged previous summer.

Summer. Begins Benjamin Moore series, named after Benjamin Moore alkyd paint used. Titles—e.g., *Hampton Roads, Island No. 10*—refer to Civil War battles.

October. First trip to Europe; travels in England, France, Spain, and Morocco. In Spain is interested in the work of Zurbarán, visits Seville, Cordova, and Granada. In Morocco visits various mosques and gardens. While in Spain makes sketches for what become the series of Concentric Squares and Mitered Mazes.

October 13–December 31. *Lake City* (1960–61), from Copper series, included in *American Abstract Expressionists and Imagists,* exhibition directed by H. Harvard Arnason at The Solomon R. Guggenheim Museum.

November 7. Opening of first one-man exhibition at Galerie Lawrence, Paris, which includes work from Benjamin Moore series. In London marries Barbara Rose; Michael Fried serves as best man.

1962

February. Returns from Europe.

March 20–May 3. *Marquis de Portago,* painting from Aluminum series, shown in *Geometric Abstraction in America,* exhibition directed by John Gordon at the Whitney Museum of American Art.

April 21–October 21. *Getty Tomb* (1959), painting from Black series, included in *Art Since 1950,* exhibition directed by Sam Hunter at Seattle World's Fair.

April 28–May 19. Paintings from Copper series shown at one-man exhibition at the Leo Castelli Gallery.

Meets Jules Olitski.

May 4. At Maidman Playhouse, New York, performs as Robert Rauschenberg in *The Construction of Boston,* a collaboration by Kenneth Koch (text), Robert Rauschenberg, Niki de Saint-Phalle, and Jean Tinguely; directed by Merce Cunningham; cast also includes Oyvind Fahlstrom, Viola Farber, Henry Geldzahler, Maxine Groffsky, Billy Klüver, Steve Paxton, and the Stewed Prunes.

Summer. Begins grisaille and multicolored Concentric Squares and Mitered Mazes series. Daughter Rachel born. Begins drawings related to what will later become Irregular Polygon series.

October 16–November 7. Grisaille paintings shown with John Chamberlain's black-and-white sculpture in two-man exhibition at the Leo Castelli Gallery.

1963

February. Paintings from multicolored Concentric Squares and Mitered Mazes series completed during winter shown in first one-man exhibition at the Ferus Gallery, Los Angeles.

May 19–September 15. *Tuxedo Park* (1959), *Pagosa Springs* (1960), *Newstead Abbey* (1960), *Cipango* (1962), and *Jasper's Dilemma* (1962–63) included in *Toward a New Abstraction,* exhibition directed by Alan Solomon at The Jewish Museum, New York.

Summer. Artist-in-residence at Dartmouth College, Hanover, New Hampshire. Teaches advanced painting students. Paints Dartmouth series, which includes metallic Valparaiso paintings and cross- and star-shaped red lead and zinc chromate paintings named after cities in Florida.

August 10–September 12. Paintings from Dartmouth series shown with sculpture of Tal Streeter, also artist-in-residence, at two-man exhibition at Hopkins Art Center, Dartmouth College.

Fall. With Henry Geldzahler, curator at The Metropolitan Museum of Art, travels in Iran as guest of Mr. and Mrs. Stanley Woodward, directors of a foundation concerned with placing modern art in American embassies.

Returns to New York; paints Purple series. Titles—e.g., *Henry Garden, Sidney Guberman*—are names of friends.

December 12–February 5. *Zambesi* (1959) and *Gezira* (1960) included in *Black and White,* exhibition directed by Alan Solomon at The Jewish Museum.

1964

January 4–February 6. Work from Purple series shown at one-man exhibition at the Leo Castelli Gallery.

February–March. With Donald Judd and Dan Flavin tapes interview by Bruce Glaser, broadcast in March over WBAI-FM (New York), with Dan Flavin omitted, under title "New Nihilism or New Art?"

April 23–June 7. *Marquis de Portago* (1960), *D* (1963), and *Henry Garden* (1963) included in *Post Painterly Abstraction,* exhibition directed by Clement Greenberg at the Los Angeles County Museum of Art.

Begins Moroccan series; titles—e.g., *Marrakech, Fez*—are names of cities in Morocco.

May 12–June 2. Paintings from Dartmouth series shown at one-man exhibition at Galerie Lawrence, Paris.

June 20–October 18. Included in the U.S. Section of the XXXII Biennale at Venice, selected by Alan Solomon: *Charlotte Tokayer* (1963) shown in exhibition in American Pavilion on Biennale grounds; *Tomlinson Court Park* (1959), *Pagosa Springs* (1960), *Jasper's Dilemma* (1962–63), *Valparaiso Green* (1963), and *Marrakech* (1964) shown in *Four Younger Artists,* complementary exhibition held in former American Consulate on the Grand Canal, an official annex of the Biennale.

Begins Running V series; titles—e.g., *Adelante, Nunca pasa nada*—are colloquial Spanish expressions.

Fall. Begins Notched V series; titles—e.g., *Quathlamba, Itata*—are names of British clipper ships.

September 29–October 24. Paintings from Running V series shown in first one-man exhibition at Kasmin Limited, London.

December 9–January 3. *Kingsbury Run* (1960), *Ophir* (1960–61),

Carl Andre (1963), *Leo Castelli* (1963), and *Valparaiso Green (Sketch)* (1964) included in *The Shaped Canvas,* exhibition directed by Lawrence Alloway at The Solomon R. Guggenheim Museum.

With Henry Geldzahler selects exhibition *Shape & Structure 1965* shown January 5–23, 1965, at the Tibor de Nagy Gallery, which includes Carl Andre, Darby Bannard, Larry Bell, Charles Hinman, Will Insley, Donald Judd, Robert Morris, Robert Murray, Neil Williams, and Larry Zox.

1965

Completes Notched V series.

January. Paintings from Notched V series shown in one-man exhibition at the Ferus Gallery, Los Angeles. First trip to Los Angeles. Meets sculptor Larry Bell and art critic Philip Leider.

February 23–April 25. *Line Up* (1962) from Mitered Mazes series included in *The Responsive Eye,* exhibition directed by William Seitz at The Museum of Modern Art.

April 19. Visiting critic, Department of Art, Cornell University.

April 21–May 30. *"Die Fahne hoch"* (1959), *Union Pacific* (1960), *Lake City* (1960–61), *Cipango* (1962), *Ileana Sonnabend* (1963), and *Tampa* (1963) included in *Three Americans/Kenneth Noland. Jules Olitski. Frank Stella,* exhibition directed by Michael Fried at the Fogg Art Museum, Harvard University.

September 4–November 28. *Valparaiso Green* (1963), *Tampa* (1963), *Mas o menos* (1964), *Black Adder* (1965), *Empress of India* (1965), and *De la nada Vida a la nada Muerte* (1965) included in U.S. representation at VIII Bienal de São Paulo, selected by Walter Hopps.

Fall. Travels to Rio de Janeiro and São Paulo. Makes first drawings for what will become Protractor series.

Paints series of works whose titles—e.g., *Bam, Baft*—are names of cities in Iran. First appearance of wide bands of color—primary and secondary—in a single painting.

Begins Irregular Polygon series; first paintings with large geometric areas of unbroken color.

Gives lecture seminar and criticizes advanced painting students at Yale University.

Continues Irregular Polygon series, which consists of 4 versions of each of the 11 shapes that make up the series. Titles—e.g., *Conway, Effingham, Chocorua*—are names of hill towns in New Hampshire.

1966

Continues Irregular Polygon series.

February 24–April 9. *Chocorua I, Moultonville I, Sunapee I, Tuftonboro IV,* and *Wolfeboro IV* (all 1966) included in *30th Biennial Exhi-*

157

bition of Contemporary American Painting at The Corcoran Gallery of Art, Washington, D.C.

March 5–April 6. Work from Irregular Polygon series shown in one-man exhibition at the Leo Castelli Gallery.

March 27. Appears in television interview with Alan Solomon as part of series "U.S.A. Artists."

April 15–16. Participates in symposium *The Current Moment in Art* sponsored by the San Francisco Art Institute. *Mas o menos* (1964) and *Agadir* (1964) included in accompanying exhibition *Six from the East*, shown April 15–May 22 at the San Francisco Museum of Art.

April 15–May 8. Work from Irregular Polygon series shown in first one-man exhibition at the David Mirvish Gallery, Toronto.

Spring. Son Michael born.

September–November. *Wolfeboro IV* included in *Systemic Painting*, exhibition directed by Lawrence Alloway at The Solomon R. Guggenheim Museum.

October 14. Performs in Robert Rauschenberg's *Open Score*, a composition consisting of a tennis game played with rackets wired for transmission of sound which in turn controls lights, presented as part of *9 Evenings: Theatre & Engineering* held October 13–23 at the 69th Regiment Armory, New York City.

October 18–November 20. Work from Irregular Polygon series shown in one-man exhibition at Pasadena Art Museum.

November 11–December 3. Selection of paintings and recent drawings shown in one-man exhibition at Kasmin Limited, London.

December 8. With Roy Lichtenstein and art historians Jerrold Lanes and William Rubin participates in "The Meaning of the Formal Statement," panel discussion moderated by Annette Michelson as part of the series *The Critic's Colloquium* organized by Irving Sandler and held November 1966–January 1967 at the Loeb Student Center, New York University.

1967

January. Appointed artist-in-residence at the University of California at Irvine but does not teach because of refusal to sign state's loyalty oath.

January 12–February 12. Pasadena Art Museum exhibition of paintings from Irregular Polygon series shown at Seattle Art Museum Pavilion; gives three lectures during course of exhibition.

February 7. Gives lecture, "The Artist's Viewpoint," at The Detroit Institute of Arts.

February 17–March 18. Work from series named after cities in Iran shown in one-man exhibition at Galerie Bischofberger, Zurich.

March. At Gemini G.E.L. in California makes first prints. Paints 42-foot long *Sangre de Cristo* at Costa Mesa, California.

April 28–October 27. *Wolfeboro III* (1966) included in *American*

Painting Now, exhibition organized by Alan Solomon in the U.S. Pavilion, Expo 67, Montreal.

June 28–September 24. *The Marriage of Reason and Squalor* (1959) and *Itata* (1964), a promised gift of Philip Johnson, included in *The 1960s: Painting and Sculpture from the Museum Collection*, exhibition directed by Dorothy Miller at The Museum of Modern Art.

Summer. Designs sets and costumes for Merce Cunningham's *Scramble*, performed August 5 at the Connecticut College Dance Festival, New London (repeated December 2 at the Brooklyn Academy of Music).

Completes Irregular Polygon series. Begins Protractor series. Titles—e.g., *Darabjerd, Sabra*—are names of ancient Near Eastern and Islamic cities with circular plans.

Travels in Canada. Teaches painting to advanced students at Emma Lake Workshop, summer extension of the University of Saskatchewan at Regina. Paints first works in the Saskatchewan series, which are variations of the Protractor series. Titles—e.g., *Flin Flon, Wakesiu*—are names of places in Saskatchewan.

November 9–December 17. *Tuxedo Park* (1960), *Polk City* (1963), *Quathlamba* (1964), and *Conway I* (1966) included in *Kompas 3: Paintings After 1945 in New York*, exhibition directed by Jan Leering and Paul Wember at the Stedelijk van Abbemuseum in Eindhoven, The Netherlands.

November 25–December 23. Work from Protractor series shown in one-man exhibition at the Leo Castelli Gallery.

1968

Continues Protractor series. Paintings from this series are shown at all one-man exhibitions taking place during the year.

February 28–March 31. One-man exhibition of paintings and drawings at the Washington Gallery of Modern Art, Washington, D.C.

March 7. Opening of first one-man exhibition at the Irving Blum Gallery, Los Angeles.

March 8. Opening of one-man exhibition at the David Mirvish Gallery, Toronto.

April 10. Receives Painting Citation in the Brandeis University Annual Creative Arts Awards.

May 13–28. One-man exhibition at Bennington College, Vermont.

June 27–October 6. *Tuxedo Park* (1960), *Quathlamba* (1964), *Moultonboro IV* (1966), *Bafq* (1966), *Hagmatana I* (1967), and colored lithographs made at Gemini G.E.L. during 1967 and '68 included in *4. Documenta*, Kassel.

July 3–September 8. *Turkish Mambo* (1959), *Six Mile Bottom* (1960), *Dade City* (1962), *Tuftonboro I* (1966), and *Gur II* (1967) included in *The Art of the Real: USA 1948–1968*, exhibition directed by E. C. Goossen at The Museum of Modern Art.

Fall. Designs stained glass windows which relate to paintings in the Saskatchewan series for projected building by Philip Johnson.

September 17–October 27. *Slieve Bawn* (1964), *Empress of India* (1965), 11 drawings for the Irregular Polygon series of 1966, and 8 lithographs made at Gemini G.E.L. in 1968 included in *Serial Imagery,* exhibition directed by John Coplans at the Pasadena Art Museum.

November. Gives lecture at The Art Institute of Chicago.

December 6. Opening of one-man exhibition at Kasmin Limited, London.

1969

Continues Protractor series.

January 4–February 6. *Protractor Variation I, Protractor Variation II,* and *Sinjerli Variation IV* (all 1968) included in exhibition *Three by Noland—Three by Stella* at the Art Gallery of Toronto.

Begins Newfoundland series. Titles—e.g., *Bonne Bay, River of Ponds*—are names of places in Newfoundland.

During spring semester teaches undergraduate beginners course in painting at Brandeis University.

March. One-man exhibition at the Mayaguez Campus of the University of Puerto Rico includes paintings from own collection, from earliest ''transitional'' paintings to recent work.

April 2–May 11. *Basra Gate I, Kufa Gate II* from the Protractor series, 4 versions of *River of Ponds* and 2 versions of *Bonne Bay* from the Newfoundland series (all 1969) shown in one-man exhibition, directed by William Seitz at the Rose Art Museum, Brandeis University.

October 18–February 1. *Zambesi* (1959), *Valparaiso Flesh and Green* (1963), *Nunca pasa nada* (1964), *Ossipee I* (1966), *Union IV* (1966), *Sangre de Cristo* (1967), *Hagmatana II* (1967), *Sinjerli Variation IV* (1968), and *Ctesiphon III* (1968) included in *New York Painting and Sculpture: 1940–1970,* exhibition directed by Henry Geldzahler at The Metropolitan Museum of Art.

November 4. Opening of one-man exhibition at the Irving Blum Gallery, Los Angeles.

November 18–December 6. One-man exhibition at the Leo Castelli Gallery includes work from Protractor and Saskatchewan series.

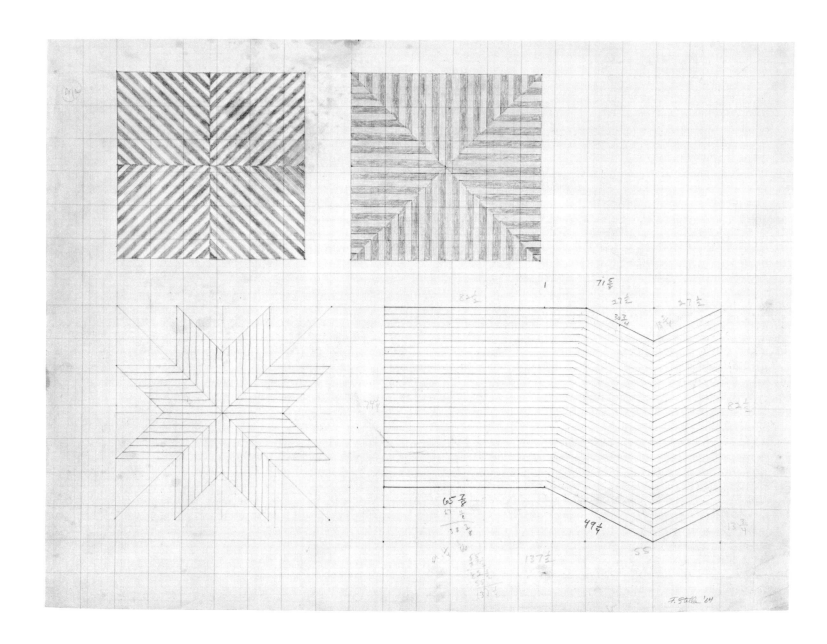

Untitled. 1964. Pencil and colored pencil on graph paper, 17⅛″ x 22″.

Bibliography

Compiled by Carolyn Lanchner

An asterisk before an entry indicates that the material has not been available for examination.

Statements, Writings, Interviews, Letters by the Artist
(arranged chronologically)

1 "An Artist Writes To Correct and Explain." Letter to the *New York Herald Tribune,* December 27, 1959, sec. 4, p. 7.
Reply to Emily Genauer, bibl. 62.

2 Lecture delivered at Pratt Institute, New York, January [or February] 1960.
Published as appendix to bibl. 55.

3 "New Nihilism or New Art?" Interview by Bruce Glaser with Stella and Donald Judd, taped February 15, 1964, broadcast over WBAI-FM (New York) March 1964.
Tape (AL 26–28) in the files of WBAI. – Published (ed. Lucy R. Lippard) in *Art News* (New York), Sept. 1966, pp. 55–61; reprinted in bibl. 12, pp. 148–64.

4 Interview by Alan Solomon with Stella and Larry Poons. Part of series "U.S.A. Artists," telecast on Channel 13 (New York) March 27, 1966.
Transcript in the files of National Educational Television, New York.

5 "The Current Moment in Art: View One." Panel discussion including Larry Poons and Roy Lichtenstein, moderated by Henry Geldzahler, April 15, 1966.
Part of symposium sponsored by the San Francisco Art Institute, April 15–17, 1966. – Broadcast over KPFA (Berkeley) Aug. 1966. – Tape in the files of The Museum of Modern Art.

6 "Conversations: Philip Leider . . . talks with Frank Stella." April 16, 1966.
Discussion group in symposium sponsored by the San Francisco Art Institute, April 15–17, 1966. – Broadcast over KPFA (Berkeley) Aug. 1966. – Tape in the files of The Museum of Modern Art.

General References (Articles and Books)

7 ARNASON, H. HARVARD. *History of Modern Art.* New York: Harry N. Abrams, 1968, pp. 621–26.
See also bibl. 67.

8 *Art Criticism in the Sixties.* New York: October House, 1967. Papers by Barbara Rose, Michael Fried, Max Kozloff, and Sidney Tillim delivered at a symposium at the Poses Institute of Fine Arts, Brandeis University, May 7, 1966. Introduction by William C. Seitz, who served as moderator.

9 "Art for Everyday Living: Painted Furs," *Art in America* (New York), October 1963, p. 97.

10 ASHTON, DORE. "U.S.A. Nouvelles explorations de l'éspace," *XXe Siècle* (Paris), June 1967, pp. 7–10.
See also bibl. 73, 114.

11 BANNARD, WALTER DARBY. "Notes on American Painting of the Sixties," *Artforum* (New York), January 1970, pp. 40–45.

12 BATTCOCK, GREGORY, ed. *Minimal Art. A Critical Anthology.* New York: E. P. Dutton, 1968, pp. 37–60, 116–64, 274–97.

BREESKIN, ADELYN. See bibl. 79.

CALAS, NICOLAS. See bibl. 144.

13 CANADAY, JOHN. "It Talks Good/Story-Telling Is Taboo, but Painting Today Is an Adjunct to Words!" *New York Times,* March 6, 1960, sec. 2, p. 13.
Discussion of Leo Steinberg's remarks in series of lectures at The Museum of Modern Art, bibl. 41.
See also bibl. 63.

COE, RALPH T. See bibl. 117.

14 CONSTABLE, ROSALIND. "The Mid 60s/Art. Is It Painting or Is It Sculpture?" *Life International* (Paris), December 20, 1965, pp. 131–34.

COPLANS, JOHN. See bibl. 90, 144.

DONNELLY, TIM. See bibl. 62.

15 FRIED, MICHAEL. "Art and Objecthood," *Artforum* (Los Angeles), June 1967, pp. 12–23.
Reprinted in bibl. 12, pp. 116–47.

16 ———. "Jules Olitski's New Paintings," *Artforum* (Los Angeles), November 1965, pp. 36–40.
See also bibl. 8, 73, 87, 98.

GASSIOT-TALABOT, GERALD. See bibl. 92.

GELDZAHLER, HENRY. See bibl. 166.

GENAUER, EMILY. See bibl. 62, 63, 67.

GOOSSEN, E. C. See bibl. 142.

GORDON, JOHN. See bibl. 68.

17 GOTTLIEB, CARLA. "The Pregnant Woman, the Flag, the Eye: Three New Themes in Twentieth-Century Art," *Journal of Aesthetics and Art Criticism* (Cleveland), Winter 1962, pp. 177–87.

18 GREENBERG, CLEMENT. "After Abstract Expressionism," *Art International* (Zurich), October 25, 1962, pp. 24–32.
   Revised and reprinted in bibl. 166, pp. 360–71.
See also bibl. 90.

GRUEN, JOHN. See bibl. 97.

HOLZ, HANS HEINZ. See bibl. 135.

HOPPS, WALTER. See bibl. 100.

19 HAMILTON, GEORGE HEARD. "Painting in Contemporary America," *Burlington Magazine* (London), May 1960, pp. 192–97.

HELLER, BEN. See bibl. 77, 84.

20 HESS, THOMAS B. "You Can Hang It in the Hall," *Art News* (New York), April 1965, pp. 41–43, 49.

HUNTER, SAM. See bibl. 70, 82.

JUDD, DONALD. See bibl. 86.

21 JURGEN-FISCHER, KLAUS. "Neue Abstraktion," *Das Kunstwerk* (Baden-Baden and Krefeld), vol. 18, no. 10–12, April-June 1965.
   Entire issue devoted to the new abstraction; comment on Stella by Michael Fried, p. 125.

KEMPAS, THOMAS. See bibl. 135.

22 KOZLOFF, MAX. "Critical Schizophrenia and the Intentionalist Method," in Gregory Battcock, ed., *The New Art. A Critical Anthology.* New York: E. P. Dutton, 1966.
   A lecture presented at the symposium "The Critic and the Visual Arts," Boston, April 1965. – Reprinted in bibl. 23, pp. 301–12.

23 ———. *Renderings. Critical Essays on a Century of Modern Art.* New York: Simon and Schuster, 1968, pp. 264–79, 301–12.
See also bibl. 8, 68.

24 KRAUSS, ROSALIND E. *Jules Olitski / Recent Paintings* (exhibition catalogue). Philadelphia, University of Pennsylvania, Institute of Contemporary Art, February 21–March 26, 1968.

25 ———. "On Frontality," *Artforum* (New York), May 1968, pp. 40–46.

LASSAIGNE, JACQUES. See bibl. 100.

LEERING, J. See bibl. 127.

LEON, DENIS. See bibl. 62.

26 LEIDER, PHILIP. "Gallery 68, High Art and Low Art," *Look* (New York), January 9, 1968, pp. 13–21.

27 "Leo Castelli, New York: La sua Storia, La sua Galleria," *Domus* (Milan), September 1963, pp. 43–48.

28 LIPPARD, LUCY R. "The Third Stream: Constructed Paintings and Painted Structures," *Art Voices* (New York), vol. 4, no. 2, Spring 1965, pp. 44–49.
See also bibl. 3, 115, 124, 130.

29 LORD, BARRY. "Spring '67: Shape of the Season," *Artscanada* (Toronto), vol. 24, no. 109/110, supplement 2, June/July 1967, p. 2.

30 *New York: The New Art Scene.* Photographs by Ugo Mulas. Text by Alan Solomon. New York: Holt, Rinehart, Winston, 1967, pp. 290–305.

31 NODELMAN, SHELDON. "Sixties Art: Some Philosophical Perspectives," *Perspecta 11* (New Haven), 1967, pp. 72–89.

O'DOHERTY, BRIAN. See bibl. 77.

PRESTON, STUART. See bibl. 62.

RAYNOR, VIVIEN. See bibl. 73.

32 ROBINS, CORINNE. "Circle in Orbit," *Art in America* (New York), November 1968, pp. 62–69.

33 ROSE, BARBARA. *A New Aesthetic* (exhibition catalogue). Washington, D.C., The Washington Gallery of Modern Art, May 6–June 25, 1967.

34 ———. "ABC Art," *Art in America* (New York), October-November 1965, pp. 57–69.
   Reprinted in bibl. 12, pp. 274–97.

35 ———. "Abstract Illusionism," *Artforum* (New York), October 1967, pp. 33–37.

36 ———. *American Art Since 1900.* New York: Frederick A. Praeger, 1967.

37 ———. *American Painting,* vol. II: *The 20th Century.* Lausanne: Skira, 1969.
See also bibl. 8.

ROTERS, EBERHARD. See bibl. 135.

38 RUBIN, WILLIAM. "Younger American Painters," *Art International* (Zurich), January 1960, pp. 25–30.

39 SANDLER, IRVING H. "The New Cool Art," *Art in America* (New York), February 1965, pp. 96–101.
See also bibl. 73, 115.

40 SEITZ, WILLIAM C. "The New Perceptual Art," *Vogue* (New York), February 15, 1965, pp. 79–80, 142–43.
See also bibl. 8, 98.

SOLOMON, ALAN. See bibl. 30, 92, 131, 152.

41 STEINBERG, LEO. "Contemporary Art and the Plight of Its Public." Lecture given at The Museum of Modern Art, February 17, 1960.
Tape in the files of The Museum of Modern Art. – Abbreviated versions published in *Harper's Magazine* (New York), March 1962, pp. 31–39, and in Gregory Battcock, ed., *The New Art. A Critical Anthology.* New York: E. P. Dutton, 1966, pp. 27–48, do not contain the references to Stella.

SWENSON, G. R. See bibl. 69, 115.

42 TILLIM, SIDNEY. "The New Avant Garde," *Arts* (Middlesex, N.J.), February 1964, pp. 18–21.
See also bibl. 8.

WHITTET, G. S. See bibl. 100.

Articles and Monographs

ANDRE, CARL. See bibl. 59.

43 ANDREAE, CHRISTOPHER. Frank Stella, *Christian Science Monitor* (Boston), September 23, 1968, p. 8.

ASHBERY, JOHN. See bibl. 169.

ASHTON, DORE. See bibl. 176.

BARO, GENE. See bibl. 174.

BATTCOCK, GREGORY. See bibl. 182.

BOCHNER, MEL. See bibl. 176.

44 BOURDON, DAVID. "New Cut in Art," *Life* (New York), January 19, 1968, pp. 44–58.
See also bibl. 176.

45 CALAS, NICOLAS. "Frank Stella, the Theologian," *Arts* (New York), December 1969/January 1970, pp. 29–31.

CAMPBELL, LAWRENCE. See bibl. 170, 176.

CASTLE, FREDERICK. See bibl. 182.

46 CONE, JANE HARRISON. "Frank Stella's New Paintings," *Artforum* (New York), December 1967, pp. 34–41.

47 CREELEY, ROBERT. "Frank Stella: A Way To Go," *Lugano Review* (Lugano), Summer 1965, pp. 189–97.

CURJEL, HANS. See bibl. 180.

DE MOTT, HELEN. See bibl. 168.

DAVIS, DOUGLAS. See bibl. 183.

DRISCOLL, EDGAR J., JR. See bibl. 190.

FACTOR, DONALD. See bibl. 171.

FISCHER, JOHN. See bibl. 182.

48 "Frank Stella, Intellectual Precisionist," in "People Are Talking About," *Vogue* (New York), November 15, 1969, pp. 114–17, 160.

FRIED, MICHAEL. See bibl. 21, 77, 99, 178.

GENAUER, EMILY. See bibl. 172.

GIULIANO, CHARLES. See bibl. 190.

GOLD, BARBARA. See bibl. 183.

GRUEN, JOHN. See bibl. 172, 176.

JUDD, DONALD. See bibl. 170.

49 KANE, GEORGE. "Stripes and Shapes by Stella," *Boston Sunday Globe, Sunday Magazine,* July 14, 1968, pp. 28–32.

KENEDY, R. C. See bibl. 188.

50 KEY, DONALD. "Stripe Painting Has Been Rough Road," *Milwaukee Journal,* June 12, 1960.

KOZLOFF, MAX. See bibl. 172, 176, 182.

KRAMER, HILTON. See bibl. 176, 182.

KRAUSS, ROSALIND. See bibl. 176.

LANES, JERROLD. See bibl. 182.

LANGSNER, J. See bibl. 171.

51 LEIDER, PHILIP. "Frank Stella," *Artforum* (San Francisco), June 1965, pp. 24–26
See also bibl. 100, 175.

52 LIVINGSTON, JANE. "Frank Stella, Lithographs, Gemini," *Artforum* (New York), November 1967, pp. 66–67.

LIPPARD, LUCY R., See bibl. 172.

53 LUCIE-SMITH, EDWARD. "Studies in Severity," *Art and Artists* (London), November 1966, pp. 55–57.

LYNTON, NORBERT. See bibl. 174.

MARMER, NANCY. See bibl. 175.

MASHECK, J. See bibl. 188.

O'DOHERTY, BRIAN. See bibl. 172.

PERREAULT, JOHN. See bibl. 182.

PETERSEN, VALERIE. See bibl. 168.

PICARD, LIL. See bibl. 168.

PINCUS-WITTEN, ROBERT. See bibl. 192.

PRESTON, STUART. See bibl. 168.

54 ROSENBLUM, ROBERT. "Frank Stella," *Vogue* (New York), November 15, 1969, pp. 116–17, 160.

55 ———. *Frank Stella* (Penguin New Art, 1). Baltimore: Penguin Books, [1970].

56 ———. "Frank Stella. Five Years of Variations on an Irreducible Theme," *Artforum* (San Francisco), March 1965, pp. 21–25.

RUIZ DE LA MATA, ERNESTO J. See bibl. 189.

SANDLER, IRVING H. See bibl. 168.

SEITZ, WILLIAM C. See bibl. 190.

57 Stella's Art Takes a New Shape (Russian text), *America Illustrated* (Washington, D.C.), December 1968, pp. 4–9.
Published by USIA exclusively for distribution abroad; Russian issue no. 146, Polish issue no. 119.

SWENSON, G. R. See bibl. 172.

Exhibitions, including reviews
(arranged chronologically)

A. Group Exhibitions

58 NEW YORK. TIBOR DE NAGY GALLERY. *Selections,* April 7–25, 1959.

59 OBERLIN, OHIO. OBERLIN COLLEGE, ALLEN MEMORIAL ART MUSEUM. *Three Young Americans,* May 11–30, 1959.
Exhibition also included Jerrold Davis and B. Pickard Pritchard. – Catalogue (in Allen Memorial Art Museum *Bulletin,* Fall, 1959, pp. 15–19) contains an unsigned statement on Stella by Carl Andre.

60 NEW YORK. LEO CASTELLI GALLERY. *Opening of the New Gallery,* October 6–17, 1959.

61 NEW YORK. NATIONAL ARTS CLUB. *Metropolitan Young Artists Show,* December 9, 1959–January 7, 1960.

62 NEW YORK. THE MUSEUM OF MODERN ART. *Sixteen Americans,* December 16, 1959–February 14, 1960.
Catalogue contains slightly revised version of Carl Andre

statement in bibl. 59. – Rev.: Emily Genauer, "16-Artist Show Is On Today at Museum of Modern Art," *New York Herald Tribune,* Dec. 16, 1959, p. 26; *idem.,* "Art," *New York Herald Tribune,* Dec. 20, 1959, sec. 4, p. 3; "The Higher Criticism," *Time* (New York), Jan. 11, 1960, p. 59; Stuart Preston, "Art: Sixteen Americans," *New York Times,* Dec. 16, 1959, p. 50; *idem.,* "The Shape of Things To Come," *New York Times,* Dec. 20, 1959, sec. 2, p. 11; Denis Leon, "Melting Pot/'16 Americans' on View," *Philadelphia Inquirer,* Dec. 27, 1959; Tim Donnelly, "But Is that Avalanche on Everest Really Necessary?" *Washington News* (Washington, D. C.), Feb. 9, 1960.

63 NEW YORK. THE MUSEUM OF MODERN ART. *Recent Acquisitions,* December 19, 1960–February 12, 1961.
Rev.: John Canaday, "Art: Miniature of Contemporary Movements," *New York Times,* Dec. 21, 1960, p. 40; Emily Genauer, "Modern Art Museum's New Show Presents A 12-Foot Pin Stripe Canvas It Calls 'Exciting,'" *New York Herald Tribune,* Dec. 21, 1960, p. 23; "'It's Exciting,'" *Newsweek,* Jan. 9, 1961, p. 78.

64 NEW YORK. LEO CASTELLI GALLERY. *Summary 1959–1960,* May 31–June 25, 1960.

65 NEW YORK. LEO CASTELLI GALLERY. *Group Show,* September 22–October 14, 1961.

66 AKRON, OHIO. AKRON ART INSTITUTE. *Explorers of Space,* October 8–November 13, 1961.
Exhibition sponsored by The American Federation of Arts, also shown at: J. B. Speed Art Museum, Louisville, Ky., Dec. 4–25, 1961; Morse Gallery, Rollins College, Winter Park, Fla., Jan. 8–28, 1962; Stanford University, Stanford, Calif., Feb. 11–Apr. 4, 1962; and Contemporary Art Association of Houston, Tex., Apr. 17–May 7, 1962.

67 NEW YORK. THE SOLOMON R. GUGGENHEIM MUSEUM. *American Abstract Expressionists and Imagists,* October 13–December 31, 1961.
Catalogue text by H. Harvard Arnason. – Rev.: Emily Genauer, "Isms Die in Their Fashion," *New York Herald Tribune,* Oct. 15, 1961, sec. 4, p. 10.

68 NEW YORK. WHITNEY MUSEUM OF AMERICAN ART. *Geometric Abstraction in America,* March 20–May 13, 1962.
Catalogue essay by John Gordon. – Rev.: Max Kozloff, "Art," *Nation* (New York), Apr. 21, 1962, pp. 364–66.

69 NEW YORK. LEO CASTELLI GALLERY. *Group Show,* April 7–21, 1962.
Rev.: G.R. Swenson, "Reviews and Previews," *Art News* (New York), May 1962, pp. 55–56.

70 SEATTLE WORLD'S FAIR. *Art Since 1950, American and International,* April 21–October 21, 1962.
Introduction to American section by Sam Hunter. – Also shown at the Rose Art Museum, Brandeis University, Waltham, Mass., Nov. 21–Dec. 23, 1962.

71 NEW YORK. LEO CASTELLI GALLERY. *Drawings,* May 26–June 30, 1962.

72 NEW YORK. LEO CASTELLI GALLERY. *Group Show,* September 22–October 13, 1962.

73 NEW YORK. LEO CASTELLI GALLERY. *John Chamberlain / Frank Stella,* October 16–November 7, 1962.
Rev.: Dore Ashton, ''New York Commentary,'' *Studio* (London), Feb. 1963, p. 67; Michael Fried, ''New York Letter,'' *Art International* (Zurich), Nov. 25, 1962, p. 54; Vivien Raynor, ''In the Galleries,'' *Arts* (Middlesex, N. J.), Dec. 1962, p. 46; Irving H. Sandler, ''Reviews and Previews,'' *Art News* (New York), Dec. 1962, p. 54.

74 THE ART INSTITUTE OF CHICAGO. *66th Annual American Exhibition,* January 11–February 10, 1963.

75 WASHINGTON, D.C. THE CORCORAN GALLERY OF ART. *The 28th Biennial Exhibition of Contemporary American Painting,* January 18–March 3, 1963.

76 NEW YORK. LEO CASTELLI GALLERY. *Group Show,* April 2–25, 1963.

77 NEW YORK. THE JEWISH MUSEUM. *Toward a New Abstraction,* May 19–September 15, 1963.
Catalogue introduction by Ben Heller; entry on Stella by Michael Fried. – Rev.: Brian O'Doherty, ''Abstract Confusion,'' *New York Times,* June 2, 1963, sec. 2, p. 11.

78 NEW YORK. LEO CASTELLI GALLERY. *Drawings,* May 20–June 29, 1963.

79 WASHINGTON, D.C. WASHINGTON GALLERY OF MODERN ART. *Formalists,* June 6–July 7, 1963.
Catalogue introduction by Adelyn Breeskin.

80 LAUSANNE. LE MUSÉE CANTONAL DES BEAUX-ARTS. *Ier Salon International de Galeries Pilotes,* June 20–October 6, 1963.
Catalogue with commemorative documentation published by the Musée Cantonal des Beaux-Arts, 1964.

81 HANOVER, NEW HAMPSHIRE. DARTMOUTH COLLEGE, HOPKINS ART CENTER. *Tal Streeter / Frank Stella,* August 10–September 12, 1963.

82 UTICA, NEW YORK. MUNSON-WILLIAMS-PROCTOR INSTITUTE. *New Directions in American Painting,* December 1, 1963–January 5, 1964.
Catalogue introduction by Sam Hunter. – Exhibition organized by the Poses Institute of Fine Arts, Brandeis University, also shown at: Isaac Delgado Museum of Art, New Orleans, La., Feb. 7–Mar. 8; Atlanta Art Association, Ga., Mar. 18–Apr. 22; J. B. Speed Art Museum, Louisville, Ky., May 4–June 7; Washington University in St. Louis, Mo., Oct. 5–30; and Detroit Institute of Arts, Mich., Nov. 10–Dec. 6.

83 NEW YORK. WHITNEY MUSEUM OF AMERICAN ART. *Annual Exhibition 1963. Contemporary American Painting,* December 11, 1963–February 2, 1964.

84 NEW YORK. THE JEWISH MUSEUM. *Black and White,* December 12, 1963–February 5, 1964.
Catalogue essay by Ben Heller.

85 LOS ANGELES. FERUS GALLERY. *A View of New York Painting, Including Major Work by Jasper Johns, Robert Rauschenberg, Andy Warhol, Ellsworth Kelly, Frank Stella, Roy Lichtenstein and Larry Poons,* January 1964.

86 HARTFORD, CONNECTICUT. WADSWORTH ATHENEUM. *Black, White and Gray,* January 9–February 9, 1964.
Rev.: Donald Judd, ''Black, White and Gray,'' *Arts,* (Middlesex, N.J.), March 1964, pp. 36–38.

87 NEW YORK. SIDNEY JANIS GALLERY. *The Classic Spirit in 20th-Century Art,* February 4–29, 1964.
Rev.: Michael Fried, ''New York Letter,'' *Art International* (Lugano), April 25, 1964, pp. 58–59.

88 NEW YORK. LEO CASTELLI GALLERY. *Group Show,* February 8–March 12, 1964.

89 PHILADELPHIA. UNIVERSITY OF PENNSYLVANIA, INSTITUTE OF CONTEMPORARY ART. *The Atmosphere of '64,* April 17–June 1, 1964.

90 LOS ANGELES COUNTY MUSEUM OF ART. *Post Painterly Abstraction,* April 23–June 7, 1964.
Catalogue introduction by Clement Greenberg (reprinted in *Art International* [Lugano], Summer 1964, pp. 63–64). – Exhibition also shown at: Walker Art Center, Minneapolis, Minn., Jul. 13–Aug. 16; Art Gallery of Toronto, Nov. 20–Dec. 20. – Rev.: John Coplans, ''Post-Painterly Abstraction: The Long-Awaited Greenberg Exhibition Fails To Make Its Point,'' *Artforum* (San Francisco), Summer 1964, pp. 4–9.

91 NEW YORK. LEO CASTELLI GALLERY. *Group Show,* June 6–30, 1964.

92 VENICE. XXXII BIENNALE. *Four Germinal Painters . . . Four Younger Artists . . .,* June 20–October 18, 1964.

U.S. representation selected by The Jewish Museum under the direction of Alan Solomon comprised 2 exhibitions: Morris Louis, Kenneth Noland, Robert Rauschenberg, and Jasper Johns were shown in *Four Germinal Painters;* John Chamberlain, Claes Oldenburg, Jim Dine, and Stella, in *Four Younger Artists.* – Catalogue essay by Alan R. Solomon. – Rev.: Gerald Gassiot-Talabot, "La Panoplie de l'oncle Sam à Venise," *Aujourd'hui, Art et Architecture* (Paris), Oct. 1964, pp. 30–32.

93 BOSTON. INSTITUTE OF CONTEMPORARY ART. *The Biennale Eight (U.S.A.),* June 20–July 26, 1964.

94 DAYTON ART INSTITUTE, OHIO. *An International Selection 1964–1965,* September 11–October 11, 1964.

95 NEW YORK. LEO CASTELLI GALLERY. *Group Show,* September 26–October 22, 1964.

96 TURIN. GALLERIA DELLE NOTIZIE. *Noland e Stella,* November 16–December 20, 1964.
   Catalogue preface is excerpt from Alan Solomon, bibl. 92. – Rev.: "La Galleria 'Notizie di Torino' presenta: Kenneth Noland e Frank Stella," *Borsa d'Arte* (Turin), Dec. 1964, p. 4.

97 NEW YORK. THE SOLOMON R. GUGGENHEIM MUSEUM. *The Shaped Canvas,* December 9, 1964–January 3, 1965.
   Catalogue text by Lawrence Alloway. – Rev.: John Gruen, "The Canvas Shape-Up," *Sunday New York Herald Tribune Magazine,* Dec. 20, 1964, p. 34; Donald Judd, "In the Galleries," *Arts* (New York), Feb. 1965, pp. 56–57; Lucy R. Lippard, "New York Letter," *Art International* (Lugano), March 1965, p. 46.

98 NEW YORK. THE MUSEUM OF MODERN ART. *The Responsive Eye,* February 23–April 25, 1965.
   Catalogue essay by William C. Seitz. – Exhibition also shown at: City Art Museum of St. Louis, Mo., May 20–June 20; Seattle Art Museum, July 15–Aug. 23; Pasadena Art Museum, Calif., Sept. 25–Nov. 7; and Baltimore Museum of Art, Dec. 14, 1965–Jan. 23, 1966.

99 CAMBRIDGE, MASSACHUSETTS. HARVARD UNIVERSITY, FOGG ART MUSEUM. *Three American Painters/Kenneth Noland. Jules Olitski. Frank Stella,* April 21–May 30, 1965.
   Catalogue essay by Michael Fried. – Exhibition also shown at the Pasadena Art Museum, Calif., July 6–Aug. 3, 1965.

100 SÃO PAULO. MUSEU DE ARTE MODERNA. *VIII Bienal de São Paulo,* September 4–November 28, 1965.
   U.S. section selected by the Pasadena Museum of Art under the direction of Walter Hopps, also included painters Billy Al Bengston, Robert Irwin, Larry Poons, and Barnett Newman *hors concours,* and sculptors Larry Bell and Donald

Judd. – Catalogue introduction by Walter Hopps. – Preview: Philip Leider, "Frank Stella," in "United States Section, VIII São Paulo Bienal, 1965," *Artforum* (Los Angeles), June 1965, pp. 24–26. – Rev.: G. S. Whittet, "The Dynamic of Brazil: The VIII Bienal of São Paulo," *Studio International* (London), Oct. 1965, pp. 136–43; Jacques Lassaigne, "8è Biennale de Sao Paulo—8th Sao Paulo Biennial," *Cimaise* (Paris), Oct. 1965–Jan. 1966, pp. 48–53.

101 BUENOS AIRES. INSTITUTO TORCUATO DI TELLA, CENTRO DE ARTES VISUALES. *Premio Nacional e Internacional 1965,* September 27–October 24, 1965.

102 NEW YORK. LEO CASTELLI GALLERY. *Group Show,* October 2–21, 1965.

103 SAN FRANCISCO MUSEUM OF ART. *Colorists 1950–1965,* October 15–November 21, 1965.

104 NEW YORK. WHITNEY MUSEUM OF AMERICAN ART. *1965 Annual Exhibition of Contemporary American Painting,* December 8, 1965–January 30, 1966.

105 STOCKHOLM. MODERNA MUSEET. *Den inhre Och de yttre Rymden,* December 26, 1965–February 13, 1966.

106 WASHINGTON, D.C. NATIONAL COLLECTION OF FINE ARTS. *United States of America VIII São Paulo Biennial,* January 27–March 6, 1966.

107 WASHINGTON, D.C. THE CORCORAN GALLERY OF ART. *30th Biennial Exhibition of Contemporary American Painting,* February 24–April 9, 1966.

108 SAN FRANCISCO MUSEUM OF ART. *Six from the East,* April 15–May 22, 1966.
   Exhibition accompanying symposium, bibl. 5 and 6, also included Roy Lichtenstein, Claes Oldenburg, Raymond Parker, Larry Poons, Larry Rivers.

109 NEW YORK. CORDIER AND EKSTROM. *Seven Decades 1895–1965/Crosscurrents in Modern Art: 1955–1965,* April 26–May 21, 1966.

110 NEW YORK. LEO CASTELLI GALLERY. *Group Show,* June 14–30, 1966.

111 NEW YORK. THE JEWISH MUSEUM. *The Harry N. Abrams Family Collection,* June 29–September 5, 1966.

112 NEW YORK. WHITNEY MUSEUM OF AMERICAN ART. *Art of the United States 1670–1966,* September 28–November 27, 1966.

113 THE ART INSTITUTE OF CHICAGO. *68th Annual American Exhibition,* August 19–October 16, 1966.

114 NEW YORK. THE SOLOMON R. GUGGENHEIM MUSEUM. *Systemic Painting,* September–November 1966.
Catalogue text by Lawrence Alloway (reprinted bibl. 12, pp. 37–60). – Rev.: Dore Ashton, "Art," *Arts and Architecture* (Los Angeles), Nov. 1966, pp. 7–8; *idem.,* "Marketing Techniques in the Promotion of Art," *Studio International* (London), Nov. 1966, pp. 271–73.

115 TOKYO. THE NATIONAL MUSEUM OF MODERN ART. *Two Decades of American Painting,* October 15–November 27, 1966.
Catalogue essays by Irving Sandler, Lucy R. Lippard, and G.R. Swenson. – Exhibition organized by the International Council of The Museum of Modern Art, also shown at: National Museum of Modern Art, Kyoto, Dec. 12–30, 1966; Lalit Kala Academy, New Delhi, Mar. 25–Apr. 15, 1967; National Gallery of Victoria, Melbourne, June 6–July 8; and Art Gallery of New South Wales, Sydney, July 17–Aug. 20.

116 FLINT, MICHIGAN. FLINT INSTITUTE OF ARTS. *The First Flint Invitational. An Exhibition of Contemporary Painting and Sculpture,* November 4–31, 1966.

117 KANSAS CITY, MISSOURI. NELSON GALLERY-ATKINS MUSEUM. *Sound Light Silence: Art that Performs,* November 4–December 4, 1966.
Catalogue text by Ralph T. Coe.

118 SANTA BARBARA MUSEUM OF ART. *Three Young Collections. Selections from the Collections of Donald and Lynn Factor, Dennis and Brooke Hopper, Andre and Dory Previn,* January 15–February 26, 1967.

119 NEW YORK. LEO CASTELLI GALLERY. *Leo Castelli / Ten Years,* February 4–25, 1967.

120 STUTTGART. WÜRTTEMBERGISCHER KUNSTVEREIN. *Formen der Farbe,* February 18–March 26, 1967.
Exhibition also shown at the Kunsthalle, Bern, Apr. 14–May 21.

121 NEW YORK. LEO CASTELLI GALLERY. *New Work,* April 1–May 10, 1967.

122 MONTREAL. EXPO '67, UNITED STATES PAVILION. *American Painting Now,* April 28–October 27, 1967.
Exhibition organized by Alan Solomon.

123 *TOKYO, METROPOLITAN MUSEUM. *Ninth Japanese International Exhibition,* May 10–30, 1967.
Exhibition sponsored by the Mainichi Newspaper Co.

124 TRENTON. THE NEW JERSEY STATE MUSEUM CULTURAL CENTER. *Focus on Light,* May 20–September 10, 1967.
Catalogue text by Lucy R. Lippard.

125 NEW YORK. THE MUSEUM OF MODERN ART. *The 1960s: Painting and Sculpture from the Museum Collection,* June 28–September 24, 1967.

126 PITTSBURGH. CARNEGIE INSTITUTE, MUSEUM OF ART. *The 1967 Pittsburgh International Exhibition of Contemporary Painting and Sculpture,* October 27, 1967–January 7, 1968.

127 EINDHOVEN, HOLLAND. STEDELIJK VAN ABBEMUSEUM. *Kompas 3: Paintings After 1945 in New York,* November 9–December 17, 1967.
Catalogue essay by J. Leering. – Also shown at the Frankfurter Kunstverein, Germany, Dec. 30, 1967–Feb. 11, 1968.

128 STANFORD UNIVERSITY. STANFORD MUSEUM. *Young Artists of the Sixties, Paintings & Sculpture from the Collection of Charles Cowles,* November 13–December 31, 1967.

129 LOS ANGELES. IRVING BLUM GALLERY. *Paintings and Sculpture from the Gallery Collection,* December 1967.

130 NEW YORK. WHITNEY MUSEUM OF AMERICAN ART. *1967 Annual Exhibition of Contemporary American Painting,* December 13, 1967–February 4, 1968.
Rev.: Lucy R. Lippard, "Constellation by Harsh Daylight: The Whitney Annual," *Hudson Review* (New York), Spring 1968, pp. 174–82.

131 BOSTON. HORTICULTURAL HALL. *American Painting Now,* December 15, 1967–January 10, 1968.
Catalogue foreword by Alan Solomon. – Exhibition, originally shown in the U. S. Pavilion at Expo 67, Montreal, sponsored by the Institute of Contemporary Art, Boston.

132 *LOS ANGELES. CALIFORNIA STATE COLLEGE. *New Sculpture and Shaped Canvas,* 1967.

133 RIDGEFIELD, CONNECTICUT. THE ALDRICH MUSEUM OF CONTEMPORARY ART. *Cool Art—1967,* January 7–March, 1968.

134 MONTREAL. GALERIE DU SIÈCLE. *Jack Bush, Helen Frankenthaler, Morris Louis, Kenneth Noland, Jules Olitski, Frank Stella, Robert Murray,* February 1968.
Exhibition sponsored in collaboration with the David Mirvish Gallery, Toronto, and the Galerie Agnès Lefort.

135 BERLIN-ZEHLENDORF. HAUS AM WALDSEE. *Ornamentale Tendenzen in der zeitgenössischen Malerei,* March 1–April 15, 1968.
Catalogue foreword by Hans Heinz Holz, essay on the exhibition by Thomas Kempas and Eberhard Roters. – Also shown at: Städtisches Museum, Leverkusen, Apr. 26–June 3; and Kunstverein Wolfsburg e. V., June 22–July 14.

136 BUFFALO, NEW YORK. ALBRIGHT-KNOX ART GALLERY. *2nd Buffalo Festival of the Arts Today,* March 2–17, 1968.

137 BUFFALO, NEW YORK. ALBRIGHT-KNOX ART GALLERY. *Plus by Minus: Today's Half-Century,* March 3–April 14, 1968.

138 NEW YORK. THE JEWISH MUSEUM. *Suites: Recent Prints,* March 12–September 2, 1968.

139 RIDGEFIELD, CONNECTICUT. THE ALDRICH MUSEUM OF CONTEMPORARY ART. *Highlights of the 1967–68 Art Season,* June 16–September 15, 1968.

140 KASSEL, GERMANY. *4. Documenta,* June 27–October 6, 1968.

141 SCARBOROUGH, ONTARIO. SCARBOROUGH COLLEGE. *Major Works from the David Mirvish Gallery,* July 1–September 30, 1968.
Exhibition also included Kenneth Noland, Jules Olitski, and Jack Bush.

142 NEW YORK. THE MUSEUM OF MODERN ART. *The Art of the Real: USA 1948–1968,* July 3–September 8, 1968.
Catalogue text by E. C. Goossen. – Also shown at: Grand Palais, Paris, Nov. 14–Dec. 23, 1968; Kunsthaus, Zurich, Jan. 19–Feb. 23, 1969; and Tate Gallery, London, Apr. 22–June 1, 1969.

143 * OTTAWA. NATIONAL GALLERY OF CANADA. Group Show of American Art, July–September 1968.
Organized by Brydon Smith to coincide with the Seventh Biennial of Canadian Painting (National Gallery of Canada, July 5–Sept. 5, 1968, organized by William C. Seitz), also included Morris Louis, Robert Morris, Kenneth Noland, Jules Olitski, Jackson Pollock, James Rosenquist, George Segal, and Tony Smith.

144 PASADENA ART MUSEUM. *Serial Imagery,* September 17–October 27, 1968.
Catalogue text by John Coplans. – Also shown at: Henry Art Gallery, University of Washington, Seattle, Nov. 17–Dec. 22, 1968; and Santa Barbara Museum of Art, Calif., Jan. 25–Feb. 23, 1969. – Rev.: Nicolas Calas, "Art & Strategy," *Arts* (New York), Mar. 1969, pp. 36–38.

145 * LONDON, ONTARIO. UNIVERSITY OF WESTERN ONTARIO, MCINTOSH MEMORIAL ART GALLERY. *Kenneth Noland and Frank Stella—New York Painters,* November 1968.

146 PHILADELPHIA MUSEUM OF ART. *The Pure and Clear: American Innovations,* November 13, 1968–January 21, 1969.

147 TORONTO, ONTARIO. THE ART GALLERY OF ONTARIO. *Three by Noland—Three by Stella,* January 4–February 2, 1969.

148 VANCOUVER ART GALLERY, BRITISH COLUMBIA. *New York 13,* January 22–February 16, 1969.

149 NEW YORK. LAWRENCE RUBIN GALLERY. *Opening Exhibition,* February 1–26, 1969.

150 HAMILTON, ONTARIO. MCMASTER UNIVERSITY. *5 by 5,* March 1969.
Exhibition also included Olitski, Noland, Frankenthaler, and Bush.

151 HELSINKI. THE ART MUSEUM OF ATENEUM. *Ars 69 Helsinki,* March 8–April 13, 1969.

152 IRVINE. UNIVERSITY OF CALIFORNIA. *New York: The Second Breakthrough, 1959–1964,* March 18–April 27, 1969.
Catalogue text by Alan Solomon.

153 ST. LOUIS, MISSOURI. WASHINGTON UNIVERSITY, GALLERY OF ART. *The Development of Modernist Painting: Jackson Pollock to the Present,* April 1–30, 1969.

154 MINNEAPOLIS. DAYTON'S GALLERY 12. *Castelli at Dayton's,* April 19–May 17, 1969.

155 BURLINGTON. UNIVERSITY OF VERMONT, ROBERT HULL FLEMING MUSEUM. *Group Show,* April 4–27, 1969.

156 ANDOVER, MASSACHUSETTS. PHILLIPS ACADEMY, ADDISON GALLERY OF AMERICAN ART. *7 Decades: 1900–1970: 7 Group Shows—Paintings and Sculpture by Alumni of Phillips Academy,* April–July 6, 1969.

157 POUGHKEEPSIE, NEW YORK. VASSAR COLLEGE ART GALLERY. *Concept,* April 30–June 11, 1969.

158 NEW YORK. THE MUSEUM OF MODERN ART. *Twentieth-Century Art from The Nelson Aldrich Rockefeller Collection,* May 26–September 1, 1969.

159 TORONTO, ONTARIO. YORK UNIVERSITY. *American Art of the Sixties in Toronto Private Collections,* May 31–June 28, 1969.

160 NEW YORK. LAWRENCE RUBIN GALLERY. *Group Show,* June 1969.

161 TOKYO. THE NATIONAL MUSEUM OF MODERN ART. *Contemporary Art, Dialogue Between the East and the West,* June 12–August 17, 1969.

162 NEW YORK. LEO CASTELLI GALLERY. *Group Show,* June 21–August 1969.

163 NEW YORK. LAWRENCE RUBIN GALLERY. *Group Show,* September 12–October 1, 1969.

164 NEW YORK. LEO CASTELLI GALLERY. *Group Show,* September 20–October 11, 1969.

165 WORCESTER ART MUSEUM, MASSACHUSETTS. *The Direct Image in Contemporary American Painting,* October 16–November 30, 1969.
Catalogue text by John McLaughlin.

166 NEW YORK. THE METROPOLITAN MUSEUM OF ART. *New York Painting and Sculpture: 1940–1970,* October 18, 1969–February 1, 1970.
Catalogue text by Henry Geldzahler.

167 MINNEAPOLIS. DAYTON'S GALLERY 12. *Stella/Noland/Caro,* November 1969.

B. One-Man Exhibitions

168 NEW YORK. LEO CASTELLI GALLERY. *Frank Stella,* September 27–October 15, 1960.
Rev.: Helen de Mott, "In the Galleries," *Arts* (New York), Oct. 1960, p. 64; Valerie Petersen, "Reviews and Previews," *Art News* (New York), Nov. 1960, p. 17; Lil Picard, [Review], *Die Welt* (Hamburg), Nov. 24, 1960; Stuart Preston, "Housing in Art's Many Mansions," *New York Times,* Oct. 2, 1960, sec. 2, p. 21; Irving H. Sandler, "New York Letter," *Art International* (Zurich), Dec. 1, 1960, p. 25.

169 PARIS. GALERIE LAWRENCE. *F. Stella,* November 1961.
Rev.: John Ashbery, "Can Art Be Excellent If Anybody Could Do It?" *New York Herald Tribune* (Paris) Nov. 8, 1961, p. 11.

170 NEW YORK. LEO CASTELLI GALLERY. *Frank Stella,* April 28–May 19, 1962.
Rev.: Lawrence Campbell, "Reviews and Previews," *Art News* (New York), Summer 1962, p. 17; Donald Judd, "In the Galleries," *Arts* (Middlesex, N.J.) Sept. 1962, p. 51.

171 LOS ANGELES. FERUS GALLERY. *Frank Stella,* February 1963.
Rev.: Donald Factor, "Los Angeles," *Artforum* (San Francisco), May 1963, p. 44; J. Langsner, "Los Angeles Letter," *Art International* (Lugano), March 25, 1963, pp. 75–76.

172 NEW YORK. LEO CASTELLI GALLERY. *Frank Stella,* January 4–February 6, 1964.
Rev.: Emily Genauer and John Gruen, "Art Tour. The Galleries, A Critical Guide," *New York Herald Tribune,* Jan. 11, 1964, p. 9; Max Kozloff, "New York Letter," *Art International* (Lugano) Apr. 25, 1964, p. 64; Lucy R. Lippard, "New York," *Artforum* (San Francisco), Mar. 1964, p. 18; Brian O'Doherty, "Frank Stella and a Crisis of Nothingness," *New York Times,* Jan. 19, 1964, sec. 2, p. 21; G. R. Swenson, "Reviews and Previews," *Art News* (New York), Feb. 1964, p. 11.

173 PARIS. GALERIE LAWRENCE. *Frank Stella,* May 12–June 2, 1964.

174 LONDON. KASMIN LIMITED. *Frank Stella/Recent Paintings,* September 29–October 24, 1964.

Rev.: Gene Baro, "London," *Arts* (New York), Jan. 1965, p. 73; Norbert Lynton, "London Letter," *Art International* (Lugano), Dec. 1964, pp. 44–45.

175 LOS ANGELES. FERUS GALLERY. *Frank Stella in an Exhibition of New Work,* January 1965.
Rev.: *Philip Leider, "Small but Select," *Frontier* (Los Angeles), Mar. 1965, pp. 21–22; Nancy Marmer, "Los Angeles Letter," *Art International* (Lugano), May 1965, pp. 43–44.

176 NEW YORK. LEO CASTELLI GALLERY. *Frank Stella,* March 5–April 6, 1966.
Rev.: Dore Ashton, "Art," *Arts and Architecture* (Los Angeles), May 1966, p. 5; *idem.,* "Conditioned Historic Reactions," *Studio International* (London), May 1966, pp. 204–7; Mel Bochner, "In the Galleries," *Arts* (New York), May 1966, p. 61; David Bourdon, "A New Direction," *Village Voice* (New York), Mar. 24, 1966, p. 17; Lawrence Campbell, "Reviews and Previews," *Art News* (New York), May 1966, p. 22; John Gruen, "Art Tour," *New York Herald Tribune,* Mar. 12, 1966, p. 6; Max Kozloff, "Art," *Nation* (New York), Mar. 28, 1966, pp. 370–72 (reprinted in bibl. 23, pp. 264–69); Hilton Kramer, "Representative of the 1960's," *New York Times,* Mar. 20, 1966, sec. 2, p. 21; Rosalind Krauss, "New York," *Artforum* (Los Angeles), May 1966, pp. 47, 49; Lucy R. Lippard, "New York Letter," *Art International* (Lugano), Summer 1966, p. 113.

177 TORONTO. THE DAVID MIRVISH GALLERY. *Frank Stella,* April 15–May 8, 1966.

178 PASADENA ART MUSEUM. *Frank Stella/An Exhibition of Recent Paintings,* October 18–November 20, 1966.
Catalogue essay, "Shape as Form: Frank Stella's New Paintings," by Michael Fried (reprinted in *Artforum* [Los Angeles], Nov. 1966, pp. 18–27; revised and reprinted in bibl. 166, pp. 403–25.). – Also shown at the Seattle Art Museum Pavilion, Jan. 12–Feb. 12, 1967.

179 LONDON. KASMIN LIMITED. *Frank Stella. A Selection of Paintings and Recent Drawings,* November 11–December 3, 1966.

180 ZURICH. GALERIE BISCHOFBERGER. *Frank Stella,* February 17–March 18, 1967.
Rev.: Hans Curjel, "Ausstellungen: Zurich," *Werk* (Winterthur, Switz.), Apr. 1967, p. 256.

181 * VANCOUVER, BRITISH COLUMBIA. DOUGLAS GALLERY. *Frank Stella: Recent Prints,* October 9–21, 1967.

182 NEW YORK. LEO CASTELLI GALLERY. *Frank Stella,* November 25–December 23, 1967.

Rev.: Gregory Battcock, "Painting Paintings for Corners," *Westside News and Free Press* (New York), Dec. 7, 1967; Frederick Castle, "What's That, the '68 Stella? Wow!" *Art News* (New York), Jan. 1968, pp. 46–47, 68–71; John Fischer, "In the Galleries," *Arts* (New York), Feb. 1968, p. 59; Jerrold Lanes, "Current and Forthcoming Exhibitions," *Burlington Magazine* (London), Feb. 1968, p. 112; Max Kozloff, "Art," *Nation* (New York), Dec. 18, 1967, pp. 667–68 (reprinted in bibl. 23, pp. 269–73); Hilton Kramer, "Frank Stella: 'What You See Is What You See,'" *New York Times,* Dec. 10, 1967, sec. 2, p. 39; "Painting: Minimal Cartwheels," *Time* (New York), Nov. 24, 1967, pp. 64–65; John Perreault, "Blown Cool," *Village Voice* (New York), Dec. 7, 1967, pp. 18–19.

183 WASHINGTON, D.C. WASHINGTON GALLERY OF MODERN ART. *Frank Stella/Recent Paintings and Drawings,* February 28–March 31, 1968.
Rev.: Douglas Davis, "Stella: 'Only What Can Be Seen There Is There,'" *National Observer* (Washington, D.C.), Mar. 25, 1968, p. 20; Barbara Gold, "Stella Exhibits in Washington," *Baltimore Sun,* Mar. 3, 1968, sec. D, p. 6.

184 LOS ANGELES. IRVING BLUM GALLERY. *Frank Stella,* March 1968.

185 TORONTO, ONTARIO. THE DAVID MIRVISH GALLERY. *Frank Stella: Recent Paintings,* March 1968.
Rev.: Paul Russell, "Frank Stella," *Artscanada* (Toronto), June 1968, p. 45.

186 BOSTON. HARCUS/KRAKOW GALLERY. *The First Lithographic Projects of Frank Stella,* March 16–April 20, 1968.

187 BENNINGTON, VERMONT. BENNINGTON COLLEGE, NEW GALLERY. *Frank Stella,* May 13–28, 1968.

188 LONDON. KASMIN LIMITED. *Frank Stella. Recent Paintings,* December 1968.
Rev.: R. C. Kenedy, "London Letter," *Art International* (Lugano), Feb. 20, 1969, pp. 38–39; Joseph Masheck, "Frank Stella at Kasmin," *Studio International* (London), Feb. 1969, pp. 90–91.

189 * MAYAGUEZ, PUERTO RICO. UNIVERSITY OF PUERTO RICO. *Frank Stella,* March 1969.
Rev.: Ernesto J. Ruiz de la Mata, "Frank Stella," *San Juan Star, Sunday Magazine* (Puerto Rico), Mar. 23, 1969.

190 WALTHAM, MASSACHUSETTS. BRANDEIS UNIVERSITY, ROSE ART MUSEUM. *Recent Paintings by Frank Stella,* April 2–May 11, 1969.
Catalogue foreword by William C. Seitz. – Rev.: Edgar J. Driscoll, Jr., "Stella Shines at Brandeis," *Boston Morning Globe,* Apr. 15, 1969, p. 25; Charles Giuliano, "Mr. Stella d'Oro of the Art World," *Boston After Dark,* Apr. 16, 1969, p. 11.

191 LOS ANGELES. IRVING BLUM GALLERY. *Frank Stella,* November 1969.

192 NEW YORK. LEO CASTELLI GALLERY. *Frank Stella,* November 18–December 6, 1969.
Rev.: Robert Pincus-Witten, "New York," *Artforum* (New York), Jan. 1970, pp. 66–67.

List of Illustrations

Dimensions are given in feet and inches, height preceding width. A date is enclosed in parentheses when it does not appear on the work of art. Unless otherwise noted, all photographs have been supplied by the owners of the paintings and drawings reproduced. *An asterisk indicates that the painting is reproduced in color.

Acknowledgments

A monograph such as this requires the assistance and collaboration of many people. I have been most fortunate in the help I have received and the spirit with which it was given. Foremost in my list of thanks is Frank Stella himself. The hours we have spent together discussing his work have produced the documentation often cited in this volume. He has been most generous with ideas concerning the book and the exhibition which this book celebrates.

The eminent critic and art historian Barbara Rose (Mrs. Frank Stella) made numerous helpful suggestions, generously gave the time to read the typescript critically, and helped clarify a number of matters relating to both the text and the biographical outline.

Professor Robert Rosenblum of the Institute of Fine Arts, New York University, was kind enough to make available to me the manuscript and page proofs of his forthcoming book on Stella, and I want to express my thanks to him and to his publisher, Penguin Books, for their permission to quote a number of passages from it. Professor Michael Fried of Harvard University has permitted me to quote extensively from his catalogue *Three American Painters,* was kind enough to read the relevant sections of this book, and made a number of helpful observations which I have incorporated in the text. My thanks go also to National Educational Television for making available the transcript of the interview between Stella and Alan Solomon, from which I have cited liberally. Philip Leider, Editor of *Artforum,* has likewise permitted extensive quotations from that magazine.

A number of dealers who have exhibited Stella's work over the years have been kind enough to provide documentation and photographs. Special thanks are due the Leo Castelli Gallery and Mr. Castelli's assistant Elita Agee; the Irving Blum Gallery, Los Angeles; Kasmin Limited, London; and the Lawrence Rubin Gallery, New York. David Whitney has also been of particular assistance. I have also received help in the way of photographs, as well as loans for the exhibition, from Charles C. Cunningham, Director, and A. James Speyer, Curator, The Art Institute of Chicago; Willis F. Woods, Director, and Samuel J. Wagstaff, Jr., Curator, The Detroit Institute of Arts; Mrs. Chloe Hamilton Young, Curator, Allen Memorial Art Museum, Oberlin College; and Professor Juergen Schulz, Chairman, Department of Art, Brown University, Providence. Among private collectors, Mr. and Mrs. Robert A. Rowan have been especially helpful.

Angelica Rudenstine, who edited the text, went far beyond the usual functions of an editor in helping me clarify substantive questions; it was a special pleasure to have worked with her. April Kingsley, Curatorial Assistant in the Department of Painting and Sculpture, performed yeoman's duty in gathering photographs and verifying data for the biographical outline; she was also of great assistance in designing the wall structure and layout of the exhibition. Carolyn Lanchner, Researcher in the Department, compiled the bibliography and displayed an uncanny ability for turning up out-of-the-way texts. The Department of Publications has devoted much time and care to the volume. Irene Gordon, Senior Editor, while under pressure of many other obligations, did the final editing of the entire book with her usual extraordinary diligence and concern for detail.

The person who has borne the brunt of the work in the preparation of the book, as well as the exhibition, and who has not only assisted me superbly but helped keep everyone in good humor throughout is my secretary, Sharon Oswald. There is no phase of this project in which she has not participated significantly.

William S. Rubin

174